ASSESSING EMPATHY

Assessing Empathy

Elizabeth A. Segal,
Karen E. Gerdes,
Cynthia A. Lietz,
M. Alex Wagaman, and
Jennifer M. Geiger

 COLUMBIA UNIVERSITY PRESS   NEW YORK

COLUMBIA UNIVERSITY PRESS
Publishers Since 1893
New York   Chichester, West Sussex
cup.columbia.edu
Copyright © 2017 Columbia University Press

Library of Congress Cataloging-in-Publication Data
Names: Segal, Elizabeth A., author. | Gerdes, Karen E., author. | Lietz,
    Cynthia A., Author.
Title: Assessing empathy / Elizabeth A. Segal, Karen E. Gerdes, Cynthia A.
    Lietz, M. Alex Wagaman, and Jennifer M. Geiger.
Description: New York : Columbia University Press, [2017] | Includes
    bibliographical references and index.
Identifiers: LCCN 2016047016 | ISBN 9780231181907 (cloth) | ISBN
    9780231181914 (pbk.) | ISBN 9780231543880 (e-book)
Subjects: LCSH: Empathy. | Social psychology.
Classification: LCC BF575.E55 S44 2017 | DDC 152.4/1—dc23
LC record available at https://lccn.loc.gov/2016047016

Cover design: Jordan Wannemacher

CONTENTS

ASSESSING EMPATHY

1

What Is Empathy?

MENTION EMPATHY TO PEOPLE and they are likely to agree that empathy is vital to all human interactions. The importance of empathy in society cannot be understated; it is the "glue that holds communities together" and the skill that promotes "being in tune with others, coordinating activities, and caring for those in need" (de Waal, 2009, p. x). Social scientists, using research and direct practice experience, almost uniformly regard empathy as what furthers our survival and enhances our social life. "Empathy and all of its components are foundational to who we are and why we succeed as a species" (Zaki & Ochsner, 2013, p. 225).

Interest in empathy has increased dramatically in recent years. Empathy is part of our human biological and social make-up. It involves a complex interaction of physiological responses and cognitive processing, which has been neurologically identified over the past ten years (Coplan & Goldie, 2011; Decety, 2012, 2015). Social service professionals from numerous disciplines have developed a deep interest in empathy. For example, there are more than two thousand training studies outlining ways for practitioners to enhance empathy (Butters, 2010). Empathy has also drawn broader public interest. Recent popular books about empathy have targeted general audiences, highlighting the positive social impact of empathy (Pinker, 2011; Rifkin, 2009; Szalavitz & Perry, 2010). Talk of empathy has reached the highest levels of our government. In his commencement address at Morehouse College in 2013, President Barack Obama encouraged the graduates to pursue empathy as the way to succeed in the world, crediting his own success to a sense of empathy and connection to others (Obama, 2013).

In spite of this attention to empathy, ask people to define empathy or explain it in detail and there is likely to be a great deal of variation and very little specificity, even among those who cite empathy as a critical skill in their professions. This thing called "empathy" tends to be broadly interpreted and applied. "The number of competing conceptualizations circulating the literature has created a serious problem with the study of empathy by making it difficult to keep track of which process or mental state the term is being used to refer to in any given discussion" (Coplan, 2011, p. 4). If we are to arrive at a clear explanation and an acceptable definition of empathy, we should examine our current understanding of empathy and how it came to be.

In its most basic form, empathy is feeling and understanding the emotions and experiences of others. Although seemingly straightforward, this definition is full of complications. Feeling something and understanding what it means are different experiences. When you add the activity of trying to identify and understand the feeling of someone else to your own feelings and understandings in a given situation, matters become more complex, and then they become even more so if you do not know the other person or are very different from that person. The eminent social psychologist C. Daniel Batson (2011) identified eight phenomena that have been considered to express or enact empathy. They are presented in box 1.1.

In spite of the many and various definitions and conceptualizations of empathy we have, Batson (2011) found that what all have in common is that they describe a process in which "one person can come to know the internal state of another and can be motivated to respond with sensitive care" (p. 11). He suggests that the best we can do is to acknowledge and understand these phenomena, clearly identify how we are defining empathy, and then be consistent in how we apply the term. However, given that there are inconsistencies even within the same profession or in similar contexts, attempting to assess and to measure empathy is especially problematic. This book was written to address these challenges. See box 1.2 for a brief synopsis of them.

As noted in box 1.2, the multiplicity of definitions for empathy makes conducting research and comparing findings very difficult. Coplan (2011) argues for a more concise definition to be shared so that we can better analyze and evaluate empathy-related research. She posits that based on recent psychological and neuroscientific research, there are three features that dis-

BOX 1.1   CONCEPTS USED TO DEFINE OR REFER TO EMPATHY

1. Knowing another person's thoughts and feelings, also referred to as *cognitive empathy* or *empathic accuracy*.

2. Matching the physical responses of an observed other on a neural level, also referred to as *mirroring, imitation,* or *motor mimicry*.

3. Feeling the same emotions that another person feels, sometimes referred to as *shared physiology*; this is considered to be sympathy by some.

4. Mentally projecting oneself into the situation of another, which involves *theory of mind* and is sometimes referred to as *aesthetic empathy*.

5. Imagining how another is thinking and feeling, sometimes referred to as *psychological empathy, projection,* or *perspective-taking*.

6. Putting oneself in the other's place, sometimes referred to as *cognitive empathy, role-taking,* or *simulation* and often considered to be akin to "walking in someone else's shoes."

7. Experiencing distress from observing another person's suffering, sometimes referred to as *empathic distress* or *personal distress*; this can also involve a process of *emotional contagion*.

8. Having feelings for another person who is suffering, sometimes referred to as *empathic concern*; often this is equated with feelings of pity, compassion, or sympathy.

(adapted from Batson, 2011)

tinguish empathy from other emotional or mental processes: *affective matching, other-oriented perspective-taking,* and *self-other differentiation*. These concepts will be developed in more detail later in this chapter. Briefly, they include mirroring emotions between an observer and the observed other (affective matching); placing oneself in another person's situation while staying focused on the other's experiences rather than imagining how we might experience that situation (other-oriented perspective-taking); and clarity that we can share another's experiences in a connecting way, still maintain our separate identity, and not substitute our understanding of the experience for that of the other (self-other differentiation). Coplan (2011) argues that only when all three of these features are present do we have empathy.

BOX 1.2   A BRIEF NOTE ABOUT MEASURING EMPATHY

The breadth of definitions of empathy begs the question: How do we measure empathy? If there are so many conceptualizations, then assessing whether people have empathy and whether empathic abilities can change is very difficult. Critiques of empathy measures that have developed over the past thirty years center on the ambiguity and multiplicity of the term *empathy* (Eisenberg & Lennon, 1983; Gerdes, Segal, & Lietz, 2010; Pedersen, 2009; Wispé, 1986). The inconsistency in definitions leads to imprecise measurements and raises questions about their validity. In addition, the variety of definitions and operationalizations of empathy means that making useful comparisons between different research findings is difficult and even meaningless at times (Coplan, 2011; Pithers, 1999). The major assessment tools used to measure empathy that are found in the literature are reviewed in more detail in chapter 6.

Adding to the challenge in measuring empathy is the emergence of new research from cognitive neuroscience, which has mapped neural circuits that are associated with empathy (see, for example, Decety, 2011, 2015; Decety & Jackson, 2004; Shamay-Tsoory, 2011; Walter, 2012). The neural processes that have been identified as being involved in empathy have not yet been fully incorporated into measurements of empathy. This book provides the historical background for how empathy has been understood, the cognitive neuroscience that emerged in the 2000s and has reconceptualized what empathy is, and what the new science of empathy means. Included in chapter 6 are instruments to assess empathy that are based on this new science.

Differences in definitions of empathy transcend disciplines. A perspective from the humanities includes contextual elements in considering empathy to be a "social feeling" and defining it as "feelingly grasping or retracing the present, future, or past emotional state of the other." As in evolutionary biology, empathy is treated as a social skill that allows us "to engage in meaningful social interaction" (Engelen & Röttger-Rössler, 2012, p. 4).

Perhaps most compelling in conceptualizing empathy are recent contributions from social and cognitive neuroscience. Empirical evidence shows that neural networks are the pathways for empathy: "Different neural circuitries underlie our ability to share and understand other people's feelings, on the one hand, and our ability to understand action intentions and abstract thoughts and beliefs, on the other hand" (Singer & Decety, 2011, p. 561). The neurological conceptualization of empathy includes observable evidence of activation of regions of the brain that contribute to the full expression of empathy. These parts are discussed in more detail later in this chapter and serve as the building blocks for the conceptualization of empathy used in this book.

We offer these varying conceptualizations of empathy to demonstrate the breadth of interpretations of it, as well as the commonalities they share. We will also review distinct interdisciplinary perspectives and consider key differences and similarities among them. With greater understanding, we can better identify the phenomenon of empathy and include empathic training in our repertoire of helping interventions.

Although defining empathy clarifies what it is that we are talking about, it is also important to discuss what we are not talking about. A number of concepts and terms, such as *sympathy* and *compassion*, are often used interchangeably with empathy, and some are mistakenly used to mean empathy (Gerdes, 2011). Such mistaken use can lead to the misperception that one is being empathic, while in reality, that is not the case. Therefore, in addition to explaining what empathy is, discussion of what is sometimes thought to be empathy but is not, is also covered in this chapter.

HISTORICAL DEVELOPMENT OF THE IDEA
AND TERM *EMPATHY*

The concept of *empathy* was developed in the early 1900s by two psychologists, Theodor Lipps (1903) of Germany and Edward Tichener (1909) of the United States. Lipps adapted a term used in the art world, *einfühlung*, which describes how one might feel while viewing beautiful art or nature. He applied it to psychology to explain feelings one has when reflecting the feelings of another person. Tichener coined the English word *empathy* to express Lipps's psychological conceptualization of *einfühlung* by basing it on the Greek word *empatheia*, which translates as "in passion" or "in suffering." Tichener's early use of the term came to be known as the description of the psychological phenomenon of inner imitation that one person experiences while seeing the actions and feeling the emotions of another person (Davis, 1996).

Tichener's work placed empathy within the domain of psychology, giving it the focus of that discipline. Subsequently, Freudian-trained psychoanalyst Heinz Kohut (1959) influenced the prevailing views on empathy by building on Tichener's emotion-sharing model and adding cognition through introspection. This conceptualization of empathy broadened its meaning to include not just feeling, but also thinking about another's emotions.

By the mid-twentieth century, the work of Carl Rogers influenced the conceptualization of empathy by incorporating empathy itself into psychotherapy practice (Wispé, 1987). He urged practitioners to check the accuracy of their interpretation of a client's "felt meaning" in order to be clear on what the client's understanding of his or her experience might be. Although Rogerian approaches to psychotherapeutic practice were widespread, the definition of empathy was still rather vague. Hackney (1978) noted twenty-one different definitions in the counseling literature, arising from Rogers's promotion of empathy in therapeutic practice (Rogers, 1957).

During the 1980s and 1990s, social and developmental psychologists became centrally involved in discussions of and research on empathy. Research emphasized two major components, the physiological experience of feeling what another person is feeling (Batson, 1991) and the cognitive processing of those feelings (Hoffman, 1981). Added to this feeling and thinking model was awareness of the boundaries between the self and other (Batson et al., 1997) and the importance of using the skill of regulating one's emotions in the process of experiencing the feelings of others (Eisenberg et al., 1994). All of these aspects of empathy have been researched, analyzed, and evaluated. Although numerous disciplines, including counseling, medicine, social work, and of course psychology, embraced integrating the concept of empathy in their practice domains, a consistent definition or conceptualization has been lacking (Cliffordson, 2001; Pedersen, 2009; Pithers, 1999). The various understandings of empathy over time, described above, can be seen in outline form in box 1.2. The emergence of neurobiology in the early years of the twenty-first century has helped to bring some clarity to defining the concept. Advances in social and cognitive neuroscience have also contributed to shaping current discussions of and research on empathy, and consensus is beginning to evolve in these areas (Gerdes, Segal, & Lietz, 2010). These advances are discussed in more detail later in the chapter.

EVOLUTION AND EMPATHY

Although the term *empathy* evolved relatively recently, empathic attributes are likely to date back to early human history. The ability to understand what other people are thinking and feeling is key to our species' survival (de Waal, 2009). Evolution likely favored the selection of caretakers of newborns who were able to understand and respond to their needs. "When pups, cubs, calves, or babies are cold, hungry, or in danger, their mother needs to react instantaneously. There must have been incredible selection pressure on this sensitivity: Females who failed to respond never propagated their genes" (de Waal, 2009, p. 67).

In addition to improved survival rates for infants whose caretakers understand their needs, experiencing such care develops a sense of security and attachment that extends through the lifetime (Collins & Feeney, 2000). Secure attachment serves as a strong indicator of empathy. In experiments that compared people's sense of attachment with their willingness to help a woman in need, for example, Mikulincer et al. (2005) found that secure attachment promotes empathy: "Attachment security allows a redistribution of attention and resources, away from self-protection and toward other behavioral systems, including the caregiving system, which operates through such mechanisms as empathy and compassion" (p. 836). In other words, the connection between empathy and attachment is circular. It takes empathic insights by caregivers to understand the needs of those for whom they are caring; when this process is successful, deep attachments that provide security for the young can develop. Secure attachment helps people respond to the distress or needs of others without raising their own distress levels; attachment-secure people are then able to go on and develop empathic relationships; and by doing so, they promote the cultivation of empathy in the next generation. Let us next look at one of the key biological building blocks of attachment and subsequently of empathy, the ability to copy the actions and behaviors of others.

MIMICRY OR MIRRORING

Evolutionary capacity to mimic is well documented. Infants show the ability to imitate expressions and actions soon after birth (Meltzoff & Moore, 1994). The mimicry behaviors of infants have been noted in research on the response of infants who hear other infants cry and who begin to cry without any other provocation (Sagi & Hoffman, 1976). Such mimicry is often referred to as *mirroring*, which, in turn, refers to the neural process that is activated when a person observes an action being done by another person (Rizzolatti & Craighero, 2004; Rizzolatti, Fabbri-Destro, & Cattaneao, 2009). The action of the observed is neurally engaged in the observer; that is, the same neural pathways are activated, thereby creating a sensation in the observing person that he or she is actually doing the action of the observed (Gallese, 2014). More definitive documentation on this brain activity has been recorded in primates rather than humans, since techniques of invasive brain investigation used in laboratories on animals cannot be done on humans. Nevertheless, through the use of brain imaging, the neural actions of mirroring can be mapped at a broader systemic level in humans. This neural mapping work demonstrates that mirror neurons create similar physical sensations in the observer when he or she is observing the actions of another (Kaplan & Iacoboni, 2006). This neural process is typically referred to as the Mirror Neuron System (MNS) because it includes a constellation of neurons or a class of cells rather than a specific part of the brain. Although this process of imitation in the unconscious mechanism of our brains is considered a building block of empathy (Iacoboni, 2009), it is likely not enough to elicit empathic understanding (Hickok, 2008). Imitation alone does not develop an understanding of the behaviors imitated. Imagine watching two people from a distance, one of whom is slapping the back of the other. Our MNS might activate our own feeling of being slapped on the back, which alerts us to the behavior, but does not tell us anything about the meaning of the slap. A slap on the back accompanied by laughter and a smile may serve as a congratulatory action, while a slap on the back accompanied by yelling and arguments may signify a fight. Mirroring accompanied by an understanding of the context and meaning attributed to behaviors are key to empathic insight.

The role of mirroring may extend to promote prosocial behaviors, or voluntary behaviors that are beneficial to others. In experiments in which participants were mimicked by researchers and later observed in different social conditions, those whose actions were mimicked were more likely to be helpful or donate to a social cause (van Baaren, Holland, Kawakami, & van Knippenberg, 2004; van Baaren, Janssen, Chartrand, & Dijksterhuis, 2009). For example, in a social experiment conducted in one community, researchers approached strangers on the street to ask for help with directions to the local train station (Müller, Maaskant, van Baaren, & Dijksterhuis, 2012). Those participants whose body postures and facial expressions were imitated by researchers and whose directions were repeated by them were more likely than those not mimicked to actually accompany the researcher to find the train station. The researchers' interpretation of these findings was that being imitated makes people feel more similar to others and hence more connected. That increased sense of connectivity promotes prosocial behaviors toward others.

It is likely that mirroring evokes a sense of being understood. When we are expressing an emotion and sharing our feelings with someone, we appreciate when that other person expresses a deep understanding of our feelings through a reflection of what we are feeling. Imagine telling a sad story to a friend and the friend laughing in response. That would not elicit a connection, nor evoke a sense of being understood. By contrast, the attachment aspects of empathy previously discussed do contribute to a sense of connection. We feel connected to others when our feelings and experiences are understood by them, and that sense of connection encourages us to understand others. This is one aspect of the social power of empathy.

GENDER AND EMPATHY

Because of the strong link of empathy to nurturance and attachment, women are often assumed to be more empathic than men. Research varies on this, and findings suggest that there may be socialization that leads to women behaving or appearing to be more empathic than men, but not necessarily a biological difference (Ickes, Gesn, & Graham, 2000). Prinz (2011) argues that given the differences in how males and females are socialized, the differences in empathy are likely a result of the way we raise children, not biological. On the other hand, research using brain imaging suggests there may be gender differences in the neural networks involved in empathy; that is, how we process our emotions in response to others may go through different neural pathways in males and females (Schulte-Rüther, Markowitsch, Shah, Fink, & Piefke, 2008). Accordingly, females tended to activate the MNS or affective response more than males, and males activated cognitive brain processes more. That too might be an effect of socialization—of differences in how males and females are raised to perceive the emotions of others. Women may process the emotions of others more viscerally initially and men may process more cognitively, that is thinking about the emotions of others more than feeling them. The lack of a clear consensus on whether there are differences in the empathic processes or levels between genders is likely a result of the difficulty in parsing out what is biological and what is socialized learned behavior. This difficulty is also apparent when considering the impact of culture on empathy.

CULTURAL DIFFERENCES AND EMPATHY

Most research and writing on empathy and culture consider the role empathy plays in cross-cultural communications, particularly in the therapeutic environment (Chung & Bemak, 2002). The consensus is that the use of empathy to transcend cultural differences can be taught, and through openness to understanding the wide range of human experiences, therapists can be engaged in cross-cultural practice (Dyche & Zayas, 2001). In a therapeutic setting, the innate capability of the therapist to be empathic across cultures is assumed. It rests primarily on the ability of therapists to engage in perspective-taking coupled with attention to cultural diversity. Interpretation of client behaviors then falls under the realm of cultural competence, or the ability to engage with and understand clients of different backgrounds and experiences. But what about empathy between cultures in general, that is, outside the therapeutic environment?

There are two ways to consider the relevance of culture to empathy. One is to ask whether there are cultural differences in the ability to express empathy; the second is to ask whether there are differences in the cultural importance placed on empathy. The first question is addressed by de Waal (2009), who finds empathy to be a key biological trait of all humans and one that is based in earliest human development. The second involves looking at how mirrored behaviors are interpreted, and this may vary across cultures. While genetic evolution shapes the physiological experience of empathy, culturally learned thinking and behaviors shape the expression of empathic behavior (Chiao, 2009, 2011). The impact of culture on the expression of empathy is not as clear as the existence of the cross-cultural physiological ability. Thus, there is agreement that across cultures there are similar forms of social knowing that can be seen as empathy, often referred to as *trait empathy*, which is the innate capacity to be empathic. However, how that empathy might be expressed or demonstrated in each culture might differ. Hollan (2012) considers research in understanding cultural differences in empathy to be lacking. He points out that we need more ethnographic studies of empathy across various cultures in order to understand how the basic traits of empathy are manifest as social behaviors. Without more cross-cultural research, Hollan posits that we risk viewing empathy only in the context of European and North American values and behaviors. Although this may portend limits to our current understanding of empathy, it is encouraging to note that numerous studies on prosocial behaviors find similar behavior patterns among a variety of cultures across the globe (Eisenberg, Eggum-Wilkens, & Spinrad, 2015).

An interesting perspective on culture and empathy can be found in work on adult education. While empathy can help bridge cultural divides in educational settings, it can be challenging to help people learn together when there are differences in personal and social experiences and backgrounds. Kasl and Yorks (2016) describe three areas of cultural difference that affect empathy: (1) how power is held—that is, whether it is peer or hierarchically distributed; (2) how aware individuals are as to their place in the dominant culture—that is, whether societal norms are viewed as central or oppressive; and (3) the strength of emotions regarding the process of learning—that is, whether the learner is highly invested or indifferent. This framework suggests that people's place within the dominant culture and their investment in learning can impact their empathic insight. These differences in how we learn may vary by culture, further adding complexity to our understanding of the impact of culture on empathy.

We contend that the biological ability to experience the full scope of empathy is shared by all human beings, although how empathy is expressed or interpreted varies in different social situations and cultural contexts. For example, cultural stereotypes, or ways that we are taught that we are different from others, can block our ability to connect empathically. Or, we can be less interested in learning about others because we have internalized the dominant culture as our own and assume that everyone else has, too. Given such limitations, we propose that engaging in social empathy is one way to address cultural differences and confront stereotypes. While this topic is discussed in more detail later in the book, we can say for now that social empathy pays attention to context and cultural awareness, as well as to others' historical experiences of inequality and opportunity, which together can lead to greater empathic awareness across cultural divides.

AFFECTIVE AND COGNITIVE ASPECTS OF EMPATHY

Overall, the MNS and the connection of empathy to prosocial behaviors involve a combination of physiological reactions interacting with the mental processing of what is observed. The two aspects, physiological reaction and mental processing, make up the full scope of empathy. In our discussion of evolution and mirroring, we focused on the physiological and biological aspects of empathy. However, as many of the definitions of empathy indicate, empathic understanding also involves taking mental images and ideas from previous experiences and bringing them together in responding to another person. Thus it involves both physiological and psychological actions, that is, affective and cognitive processes.

Affective empathy describes the physiological aspects of vicariously feeling what another person is feeling, while *cognitive empathy* involves the mental processing of another's feelings, thoughts, or intentions (Hetu, Taschereau-Dumouchel, & Jackson, 2012; Walter, 2012; Zaki & Ochsner, 2012). Put simply, affective responses to the actions of others are unconscious; and cognitive processing of the actions of others is conscious. Although separate and operating through different kinds of brain activity, these two processes seem to occur almost instantaneously. Understanding how affective and cognitive responses build empathy can illuminate pathways for assessing and teaching empathy.

Affective empathic responses happen on a physiological level and often involve mirroring (Iacoboni, 2008). Although having the same sensations as others can help us to understand them, that alone is not a guarantee of empathy. If we see a person smiling, we may feel that sensation of smiling, but we cannot know for certain that the ideas that smiling evokes for us are the same as they are for the other person. As noted previously, empathy involves more than imitation. That is where cognitive processing plays such an important role.

Moving from experiencing what another person is feeling to thinking about it and understanding what it might mean involves the cognitive processing of empathy. When our response is triggered by an affective stimulus, we consciously try to deduce the reasons or motives for the other person's observed action. In other words, empathy engages these consecutive unconscious and conscious processes (Decety, 2015; Preston & Hofelich, 2012; Shamay-Tsoory, 2011; Walter, 2012). Although these processes have been mapped neurologically as separate actions, they feel almost seamless. For example, imagine hearing a shrill cry and feeling yourself jolted to fearful attention, and then, turning toward the noise, you see young children run by laughing. At first, your body reacted affectively to a stimulus, the shrill cry, but then your mind took in the evidence from the scene to make sense of the cry in terms of the children's behavior. You might have even smiled at the scene, remembering your own joy in playing as a child or recalling the multitude of such scenes of children interacting you have taken in throughout your life. This process of unconsciously reacting to a sound and then seeing actions that help to explain what it means likely makes sense based on your human experience. But documentation of this process in the brain has been accomplished only in recent years as a result of technological advances. Through analysis of sophisticated brain images captured by functional magnetic resonance imaging (fMRI) and other technology, neuroscience has been able to map areas activated in our brains that correspond to affective processing and cognitive processing.

A COGNITIVE NEUROSCIENCE CONCEPTUALIZATION OF EMPATHY

Based on what we have presented thus far, we can conceptualize empathy to be a process that combines different ways of knowing about other people. When these differing pathways come together, we gain empathic insight. These pathways include unconscious and conscious processing of information and involve numerous parts of our brains and nervous system. Neurologically, empathy is a "multi-component construct" involving a number of distinct neural pathways and systems (Eres, Decety, Louis, & Molenberghs, 2015). Thus, we use the concept of the *full scope of empathy* to refer to both the unconscious and the conscious aspects of empathy. Because it is difficult to articulate what the full scope of empathy means in one concise sentence, it is helpful to outline the components that together make up empathy. For that we turn to cognitive neuroscience.

Until the advent of sophisticated neuroimaging technology, research on empathy involved observing people's behaviors in experimental settings or relying on self-reported perceptions of empathy. Although both are subjective, it turns out that a lot of the observational and self-reported aspects of empathy can objectively be seen in operation in different parts of the brain. The mapping of empathy in the brain has been done through experiments using fMRIs and other advanced technologies.

Indeed, cognitive neuroscience findings from the early 2000s confirm that empathy includes unconscious evolutionary physiological survival responses and learned conscious cognitive processing. There is no specific place in the brain where empathy occurs. Different parts of the brain are involved in unconscious and conscious ways and can be observed through brain patterns that correspond with empathizing with another being (Decety, 2011, 2015; Decety & Moriguchi, 2007). Mapping brain activity has allowed neuroscientists to confirm much of what psychologists have conceptualized over the years and develop more complete ways of identifying and defining empathy.

THE COMPONENTS OF EMPATHY

Several components that together contribute to the full scope of empathy, including affective and cognitive ones, have been identified by leading neuroimaging researchers (Decety & Moriguchi, 2007). Putting together research on empathy informed by cognitive neuroscience, psychology, and social work, we have developed a model to demonstrate the affective and cognitive aspects of empathy and their possible outcomes. A full model of the process of interpersonal empathy is outlined in figure 1.1 and discussed further below.

In figure 1.1, the first column identifies the possible sources and types of stimuli that might trigger an affective or unconscious physiological response. We take in the external world through our senses, and from that we may begin to have a reaction, such as fear or happiness. Understanding what that reaction might mean for us happens through the processes outlined in the next column. We use various skills including mentalizing or thinking about what we have seen, and process those images or affective responses through several skills that together make up empathy. The key cognitive skills we use are self-other awareness, perspective-taking, and

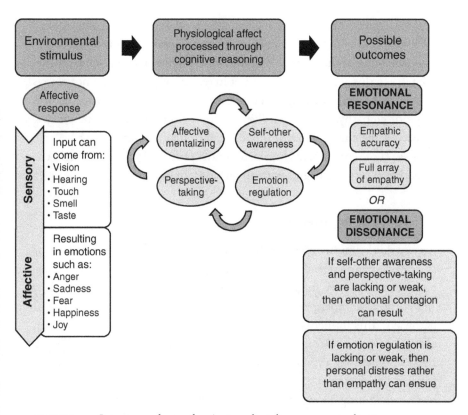

FIGURE 1.1 Interpersonal empathy: An interdisciplinary conceptualization

emotion regulation, all described in more detail in the next sections of this chapter. If we successfully engage in processing the physiological inputs through cognitive assessment, we can have several possible outcomes. The last column of figure 1.1 lists those possibilities. The top list outlines what we have when we are in sync with others and have emotional resonance. The result is empathic outcomes, that is, understanding what another is feeling based on observation of his or her actions. Sometimes we are not successful and are out of sync with others. This can lead to emotional dissonance and we may experience distress at seeing the actions or experiences of another.

Figure 1.1 outlines interpersonal empathy. By interpersonal empathy we mean empathic abilities of the individual in relation to other individuals. This is different from the concept of social empathy, which we discuss later in this chapter. The interpersonal empathy model in figure 1.1 shows a linear flow from the initial impact of an environmental stimulus to the cognitive processing of that stimulus to the possibility of an empathic response. We refer to this as a linear process, but in reality, we humans are not always so one-directional. Although all the components are necessary for the full scope of empathy, in our real lives, we may find ourselves experiencing aspects of the empathic array in a different order, or we may not become aware of those components until later in the process. Typically though, the empathic experience begins with an outside stimulus.

Affective Response

An outside stimulus may touch us through one of our senses, such as through hearing a sound or seeing an image or action. Often we experience multiple inputs—we might hear and see someone crying—and the sight and sound of another person's crying triggers activation of our own neural pathways. This immediate reaction, often on an unconscious level, is an affective response (Decety & Skelly, 2014; Fonagy, Gergely, Jurist, & Target, 2004). Sometimes a physiological input does not have to be observed to produce an affective response; that is, such a response can also be triggered by our imagining an event. The state of imagining or thinking about an experience is known as *affective mentalizing* and is also neurologically observable (Schnell, Bluschke, Konradt, & Walter, 2011).

Affective Mentalizing

Affective mentalizing is the process of cognitively appraising someone's emotional state (Frith & Frith, 2006). We infer others' emotional states through nonverbal cues (such as facial expressions) as well as knowledge about other people's situation and beliefs. When experiencing affective mentalizing, we may even have physiological reactions that mirror the imagined affect. Mentalizing can take place without much direct stimulus. For example, reading about a person's situation, or listening to someone talk about it on the phone, or hearing someone else describing that person's situation can all evoke mental pictures which can result in affective experiences. Affective mentalizing is therefore both a physiological reaction and a cognitive response. In this way, affective mentalizing serves as a bridge between affective experiences and cognitive reasoning. Thus, in the model, affective mentalizing is found under the larger task of cognitive reasoning, but is close to the affective response part of the model.

Once affective responses are triggered, the brain, when functioning fully, will start to engage other processes to try and make sense of the mirrored feelings. This effort of interpretation involves the conscious part of processing what that image or experience might mean. This process moves us from affective response to cognitive processing in the model. The cognitive processing part includes three separate but intertwined components: *self-other awareness*, *perspective-taking*, and *emotion regulation*.

Self-Other Awareness

Self-other awareness is the ability to identify with another while maintaining a clear sense of self. It requires being able to differentiate the experiences and feelings of others, as well as their understanding of those feelings and experiences, while keeping separate from one's own experiences, feelings, and understanding (Decety & Sommerville, 2003; Moran, Kelley, & Heatherton, 2014). It requires both a sense of one's own agency and insights into others'. In professional settings self-other awareness might be articulated in terms of having "strong boundaries," or being able to keep another person's feelings or situations from becoming our own. In popular self-help literature, it might be expressed in the admonishment not to become too "enmeshed" in another's situation or to keep from blurring the line between what is my experience or concern and what is yours.

In relation to empathy, it is imperative to be able to distinguish between one's own feelings and those of another (Lamm, Bukowski, & Silani, 2016). When we cannot make that distinction, we can become overwhelmed or distracted by our own emotions and shift our focus away from the other and onto ourselves. Suppose a friend calls on the phone to tell you that she is distraught because she just lost her job. Of course the friend wants you to understand how she is feeling, that is why she called. However, in addition to being understanding of our friends feelings, we also need to understand what we are experiencing. If we get self-absorbed in making meaning out of our own emotions and ignore the situation of the other, then we are not experiencing empathy. Affective response followed by poor self-other awareness can lead to *emotional contagion*, which involves unconscious mimicry and the subsequent sense of feelings that we "catch" from others (Hatfield, Rapson, & Le, 2011). Examples of emotional contagion are laughing when others laugh even if we don't know what they are laughing about, or picking up the anger of others in a crowd, again without necessarily having a personal reason to be angry. When an emotional response spreads through a crowd without knowledge of who or what is the source of that emotion, we sometimes call it "mob mentality." The distinction between the self and others when affectively responding to an external stimulus is what differentiates empathy from emotional contagion (McCall & Singer, 2013). But self-other awareness is only the first step in cognitively processing affective responses.

Perspective-Taking

The way to maintain self-other awareness and at the same time make meaning out of another's experiences is to engage in perspective-taking. Perspective-taking is "the mental flexibility to intentionally adopt the perspective of the other" (Decety, 2005, p. 144). The most common way of describing perspective-taking is "walking a mile in another's shoes." This involves the ability to imagine what it would be like to be in the situation of another person; it is a form of mentally toggling back and forth between being in someone else's situation and being in your own. However, perspective-taking without self-other awareness can lead one astray. If we do not maintain strong self-other awareness, we may be good at taking another's perspective, but we process what it means to ourselves, not to the other person. This differentiation is very important. We might feel as if we are empathic because we are taking another person's perspective, but we may introduce our own way of responding to the situation rather than stay with thinking through the situation from the other person's perspective. That introspection is not empathy, since empathy must take into consideration what an experience means to the other person. Coplan (2011) explains it well: "In other-oriented perspective-taking, when I successfully adopt the target's perspective, I imagine being the target undergoing the target's experiences rather than imagining being myself undergoing the target's experiences" (p. 13).

Related to perspective-taking is the ability to infer the mental state of others described as *theory of mind* (ToM) (Krendl & Heatherton, 2009).

ToM, also referred to as *mentalizing*, refers to the thinking that goes into trying to understand another person's behavior. Some researchers contend that it is the closest ability we have to mind-reading. Experiencing the same feelings as another, affectively reacting, is not the same as understanding the cause of those feelings. ToM involves perspective-taking as a way to understand what the other person may be experiencing, but couples it with information that we have gathered from our own experiences and that may provide insight into what is most likely to occur in such a context (Frith & Frith, 2006). Thus, ToM is part of our empathic ability because when prompted by affective reactions to others, we need to develop cognitive inferences about their state of mind in order to understand their perspective (Dvash & Shamay-Tsoory, 2014). Although ToM relies on combining affective and cognitive processes, it differs slightly from empathy in that it introduces our own thinking about situations based on our experiences. Because empathic insight draws at times on our own experiences, the distinction is indeed subtle. It has to do with self-other awareness: When we view the other's world through our own experiences, we risk misinterpreting the meaning of the experience for the other because we can never really know what the other is thinking in a given situation (Mitchell, 2009). A simple example can help illuminate this. Suppose you are sitting on a park bench and a person jogs by you. You also jog and love the feeling you have after a good run. Upon first seeing the jogger, you may have some unconscious physical sensations of running, such as elevated heart rate, breathing harder, and even the feeling of having the pavement beneath your feet. ToM would move you to infer something about the mental state of the jogger; that is, your love of jogging may lead you to think about how good the person will feel after completing the run. You will have used affective reaction and cognitive processing to infer the other's state of mind. Then the person comes to a stop and sits down next to you on the bench, muttering how hard it is to jog and swearing to never try it again. That would give you information that tells you that your inference based on your experience does not apply to the experience of the other person. This is why self-other awareness is so important. Without a strong reminder of self-other awareness, your inference may be what you would think in that situation, not what the other person is actually thinking. Empathy pushes us to remain open to other interpretations of what an experience may mean. And doing that involves one more complementary component, emotion regulation.

Emotion Regulation

Maintaining one's balance while unconsciously experiencing affective reactions and working to make sense of those feelings through cognitive processes can be challenging and overwhelming at times. Faced with being told by a friend that he has just received news that his father died can instantaneously bring you feelings you had when you heard the same news about your father (affective response) and trigger a visual memory of the room in the hospital where you received that news (affective mentalizing). Your first reaction might be to start crying, although you are aware on some level that this is about your friend's loss (self-other awareness), and not about your own. You quickly step into his shoes (perspective-taking), while thinking back to your experience and trying to say the things that would have made you feel supported (ToM). Through all these steps of empathy, you are trying not to cry and feel all those emotions you had when your own father died. At that moment, you are working to engage emotion regulation. In order to handle the intensity of feelings evoked by affective and emotional stimuli, we need to be able to regulate our emotions.

Emotion regulation as a component of empathy is the ability to react to another's experiences and process what those reactions might mean without becoming overwhelmed or swept up into someone else's emotions. Studies have shown that those who can regulate their emotions are more likely to respond to others in empathic and prosocial ways (Eisenberg, Smith, Sadovsky, & Spinard, 2004). Thus the model in figure 1.1 includes the component of emotion regulation as part of the cognitive reasoning. Emotion regulation can be seen as having a calming effect while we delve into perspective-taking and strive to maintain self-other awareness.

THE COMPONENTS OF THE FULL SCOPE OF EMPATHY

If all goes well and one is able to navigate through the processes of affective response and affective mentalizing, while maintaining self-other awareness and engaging in perspective-taking and emotion regulation, then one has achieved the full scope of empathy. This process of achieving the full scope of empathy is not a fully developed science. We know from neural imaging that all these processes involve different parts of the brain, some overlapping, some sequential, some sometimes stronger at one time than another. Recent research suggests that empathy may be better understood as an umbrella term for a collection of processes (Gentili, Cristea, Ricciardi, Costescu, David, & Pietrini, 2015). We regard that collection as consisting of the five components we have been discussing.

The expression of empathy is dynamic and changing, given varying degrees of each component, both within ourselves and according to situation. Empathy is truly a "moving target," but knowing the components allows us to identify skills and abilities and helps us to develop them. Increasing a component, or parts of several components, can contribute to empathy as a whole. Based on our professional experiences, some change or growth is better than nothing, and for many learning situations, small changes over time are the best outcome we can achieve. Moreover, they can eventually add up to big change. And in fact, often that is the best way to effect change anyway, bit by bit, as that is more likely to have a lasting impact. Hence, learning to be empathic, or more empathic, can be more clearly achieved by understanding the components that make up the full scope of empathy, and then developing each component to its fullest. It is this philosophy that guided us in the development of instruments to measure each component. These instruments are presented and fully explained in chapter 6.

SOME COMMON MISCONCEPTIONS ABOUT BEING EMPATHIC

Before moving on to the application of empathy on a broader social scale, we would like to clarify some common misconceptions about empathy. A number of different emotions and constructs have been used to describe or measure empathy, or have been used as a synonym for it. Because of the complexity of what makes up the full scope of empathy, it would make sense that there is a tendency to confuse empathy with similar or related emotions or feelings.

Personal Distress

We have already mentioned the experience of emotional contagion, or the physiological mirroring that occurs in reaction to events in ways that we are not fully aware of and cannot understand in terms of their origin or meaning. Emotional contagion is related to *personal distress*. Personal distress in the empathy literature describes the phenomenon of feeling another's pain or discomfort. In some earlier work on empathy, personal distress was considered a key component of empathy. For example, one of the most well-known instruments for measuring empathy, the Interpersonal Reactivity Index (IRI) (Davis, 1980, 1983) considers personal distress to be a part of an overall conceptualization of empathy. Over the years, though, the subscale for personal distress in the IRI has often been dropped because of findings in cognitive neuroscience research that the capacities for self-other awareness and emotion regulation are likely to be involved in differentiating between emotional contagion or personal distress on the one hand, and empathy on the other hand: "Awareness of our own feelings, and the ability to consciously regulate our own emotions, may allow us to disconnect empathic responses to others from our own personal distress" (Decety & Lamm, 2011, p. 206). Personal distress is more of an over-arousal of emotions that is self-focused (Eisenberg, 2002). With personal distress, one is more likely to avoid contact in order to not have to deal with the discomfort or anxiety that arises from the emotions of another. Such avoidance and self-focus are not empathy.

Sympathy

Although sympathy is often used by people to mean empathy, and vice versa, we know today based on neurological empirical evidence that these are distinctly different states (Gerdes, 2011). Being sympathetic may involve being emotionally in tune with another, but sympathy does not necessarily involve active imitation or mirroring and may not involve perspective-taking. "The crucial distinction between the term *empathy* and those like *sympathy, empathic concern*, and *compassion* is that empathy denotes that the observer's emotions reflect affective sharing ('feeling with' the other person) while compassion, sympathy, empathic concern denotes the observer's emotions are inherently other oriented ('feeling for' the other person)" (Singer & Lamm, 2009, p. 84). Another way to view sympathy is that it is a "third-person" emotional response, as opposed to putting oneself in the situation of another (Darwell, 1998). Sympathy also usually concerns situations that are troubling or negative for people. We can feel bad for a person, be sympathetic, without engaging any of the other components that make up empathy. In fact, because sympathy tends to reflect feeling *bad for* someone else because of the situation the person is in, we can stay removed from actually sharing feelings and instead assume a hierarchical position, one in which we are not the ones suffering or in distress at all, in contrast to the subject of our sympathy. The effect can be condescending rather than achieving and communicating true understanding.

Compassion

Compassion tends to evoke a more charitable feeling about another's woes, but it too is concerned with distressing situations. We do not have compassion for people who are happy and doing well. It is all focused on pain or distress. Compassion can involve some of the components of empathy, such as self-other awareness, perspective-taking, and even emotion regulation. It can even be triggered by affective responses that lead to perspective-taking. However, compassion differs from empathy because it does not involve a shared experiencing of another's emotions or life situation (Goetz, Keltner, & Simon-Thomas, 2010). Compassion is "the feeling that arises in witnessing another's suffering and that motivates a subsequent desire to help" (Goetz, Keltner, & Simon-Thomas, 2010, p. 351). It parallels and often coexists with sympathy, and as such, can also have a hierarchical aspect to it: We have compassion for those less fortunate or those who are suffering, often meaning we are in a better situation. It is important to note that we are not saying empathy is better than compassion or sympathy, just that these are different states and should not be confused to mean the same thing.

Judgment

Focusing on ourselves can also lead us to become judgmental: "Oh, I would never do that if I were in her situation." Although that may be a valid point and a good way to learn from the actions of others, it is not necessarily empathy. Empathy involves placing yourself in the situation of another, and, as noted before, asks you to think about what the other person is feeling or might do, not what you are feeling or might do. This distinction is also subtle, but very important. A note to those of you who may think that empathic insight means accepting all the behaviors of others: No, that is not empathy either. "Walking in another's shoes" may require effort to understand why a person may behave a certain way, but in the end, we are free to accept or reject the other's behavior as a legitimate response to something that person has experienced. An example that sometimes is used in legal defenses might help illuminate this phenomenon.

Picture the trial of a defendant who has committed a vicious crime and the defense attorney pointing to what a terrible childhood the defendant had, having been abused as a child, and suggesting that his upbringing contributed to his current violent behavior, possibly implying it was beyond his control. In light of these considerations, the attorney asks the judge to show leniency in sentencing. That scenario is asking for empathic insight into what it might have been like to grow up suffering abuse and what subsequent life experiences of the defendant might have been impacted by that abuse, and then concluding that the vicious crime was a result of that upbringing. Empathy can help us better understand what may have contributed to current behavior, but it does not mean we have to excuse that behavior. Other learned behaviors, such as obeying the law, can be expected to be followed in spite of a person's difficult childhood. Empathic insight might help us to try to change conditions for other children so that life outcomes may improve, and it might move us to find help for the defendant, but it is not necessarily a free pass to excuse away certain behaviors, particularly when those behaviors hurt others. Empathic insight produces an explanation, which is helpful as we decide how to respond; it does not lead to the conclusion that we should do nothing to prevent or to respond to violence.

It is important to fully understand what makes up the full scope of empathy because there is a tendency for people to use terms such as *sympathy* and *compassion* to mean empathy and invoke empathy in inaccurate ways. Before brain mapping became scientifically possible, we could not be as definitive about what is and is not empathy. With the ability to observe visible activity in the brain that corresponds to key behaviors that demonstrate empathy, we can better understand what it is that defines being empathic.

INTERPERSONAL EMPATHY AND SOCIAL EMPATHY

In the previous sections of this chapter, we have used *empathy* mainly as an all-encompassing term and treated it as the primary concept. But we can also further understand empathy by taking into account its personal and societal dimensions and thus distinguishing between interpersonal empathy and social empathy. When we speak of empathy between individuals, we mean interpersonal empathy, while social empathy is the application of empathy on and by larger systems, such as organizations that are responsible for decisions and policies that impact large groups of people. Both concepts share the fundamental characteristics of empathy outlined in this chapter and thus we often refer not to one or the other but to empathy in general. However, at times it is helpful to distinguish between the two dimensions of empathy.

As previously discussed, interpersonal empathy is vital to healthy social relationships. However, without a full understanding of the context of other's lives, empathic insight can be limited (Singer & Lamm, 2009). Imagine that you are visiting a new country, for example, Australia. You arrived at night, and so saw very little. On your first morning you took a stroll through a park that was across from your hotel and looked very much like ones you were familiar with at home. Then you came upon a group of men who were grabbing and pushing and jumping all over each other, with what looked like a hostile craziness. You were affectively alarmed, feeling the pushes and shoves, and cognitively confused, because while it looked like a big fight, no one seemed to be angry. In short time, you noticed a ball that to you looked similar to a football. You had stumbled across a group of people playing the game of rugby, something new to you. Although this experience of discovering the game of rugby may seem rather simple and not at all life-changing, it can be magnified by the interactions one might have over a lifetime with numerous different cultures and races, as well as visits to places that are foreign to you. One way to assimilate all this different information is to apply social empathy.

SOCIAL EMPATHY

"Social empathy is the ability to understand people by perceiving or experiencing their life situations and as a result gain insight into structural inequalities and disparities" (Segal, 2011, pp. 266–267). Figure 1.2 provides a schematic view of social empathy and its relationship to interpersonal empathy. We consider the foundation of social empathy to be interpersonal empathy, and a more detailed description of this relationship is described in chapter 5. All the aforementioned components of affective response, affective mentalizing, self-other awareness, perspective-taking, and emotion regulation not only contribute to experiencing the full

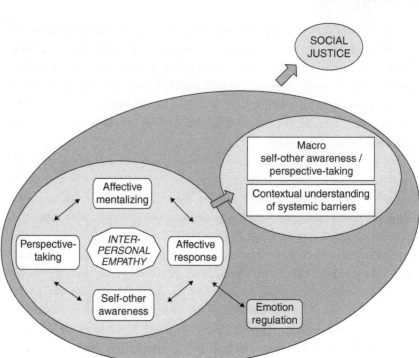

FIGURE 1.2 Social empathy

scope of interpersonal empathy, but also serve as a springboard for applying social empathy.

The larger application of empathic insights, that is, social empathy, is
accomplished through two additional components: contextual understanding of systemic barriers, and macro self-other awareness/perspective-taking
(Segal, Wagaman, & Gerdes, 2012). Both are related to key components of
interpersonal empathy, but expanded to encompass a broader scope of
information intake and understanding.

Contextual Understanding of Systemic Barriers

Complex social cues can impact our experience of empathy (Zaki & Ochsner,
2012). Social empathy includes the ability to assess a social context at a
macro level in order to fully understand the lived experiences of groups
different from our own. We need to understand the historical events that

shaped the group and contributed to its members' identities today. It is particularly important to understand historical context when that history includes oppression and barriers that prevented groups from participating in the larger social environment because the history of marginalization and/ or privilege can have a profound impact on shaping people's lives and group behaviors. Understanding this is critical to our ability to develop empathy for other cultural groups across the globe (Hollan, 2012).

To understand the diversity of contexts and cultures, we need to develop empathic skills on a broader scale. We do this by studying and analyzing sociohistorical contexts. Once we have contextual understanding, we are better prepared to engage in the other component of social empathy, macro self-other awareness/perspective-taking. In the larger context of other cultures, the macro skill of perspective-taking assumes the ability to see oneself as different from others. We engage in understanding the historical events that occurred to others because we do not share the same group experience. For this reason, macro perspective-taking assumes the inclusion of self-other awareness. Thus the macro perspective-taking skill includes applying the interpersonal skills of self-other awareness and perspective-taking on a larger cultural or societal level.

Macro Self-Other Awareness/Perspective-Taking

Although similar to the skills involved in interpersonal empathy, macro self-other awareness/perspective-taking asks us to walk in the shoes of another, but with an eye toward the impact of external factors that impact experience. By putting ourselves in the situations of others with different characteristics of group identity, such as race, gender, sexual orientation, ability, age, and class background, we can develop broader empathic insight, which is social empathy.

We know that perspective-taking can increase social bonds by building social connections and decreasing group stereotyping (Galinsky, Ku, & Wang, 2005). Applying perspective-taking across larger social groups can facilitate more positive social engagement. For example, recognition of needing a broader experiential understanding of other cultures has been introduced to the U.S. Army in order to better prepare personnel to serve in other countries. The ability to understand differences in cultures and communities and what that means to the individuals living there has been referred to as *social perspective-taking* by military trainers (Roan et al., 2009). Social empathy takes this recognition of needing a broader perspective to empathically understand other cultures and develops it based on the foundation of interpersonal empathy.

SOCIAL JUSTICE AND EMPATHY

The importance of interpersonal empathy rests on its capacity to improve relationships between people. The importance of social empathy rests on its capacity to improve the relationships and rules of behavior between different groups and cultures. We believe that building empathy across individuals and communities has the added benefit of improving social relations. This improvement can lead to a more socially just world. When empathic insight is gained, often a sense of social responsibility follows (Frank, 2001). Although this may seem like a lofty step from making sense of physical sensations we have while watching another person, it is exactly that progression of understanding that, when multiplied across millions of people and across a global span, does build a more caring and empathic world. Martin Hoffman (2000), one of the leading researchers on empathy and moral development, explains the relationship between empathy and social responsibility:

> If one thinks about how society's resources should be distributed, one might focus on the implications of different distributive systems for oneself or for others. A self-serving perspective will lead one to prefer principles that coincide with one's own condition: A high producer would choose output, competence, or effort and a low producer would choose need or equality. An empathic perspective, on the other hand, would lead one to take the welfare of others into account ... [and] that leads one to imagine the consequences of different systems for society's least advantaged people or for people who work hard. (pp. 230–231)

To apply what we now know from cognitive neuroscience to this observation, we can see that Hoffman is speaking about using skills of perspective-taking and self-other awareness on a societal level and that these lead to a sense of social responsibility. That is the foundation of our research into and application of interpersonal and social empathy. We view interpersonal and social empathy as tools for us to improve our own lives and other people's lives, as well as to promote social well-being. To achieve those goals, we need to better understand the components of empathy, and be able to better assess whether we have been successful in developing and enhancing empathic abilities. The rest of this book provides in-depth information on empathy, how we develop empathy, and tools to measure and assess empathy.

The Building Blocks of Empathy

NOW THAT WE HAVE A BASIC UNDERSTANDING of what empathy is, we can examine more closely what makes us empathic. By identifying the building blocks of empathy, we can better understand what is and is not empathy and thereby promote the development and enhancement of empathy within and between individuals, as well as in the larger society. In this chapter we explore the evolution of empathy within humanity, the biological underpinnings of empathy, and where and how in the brain we believe all this happens.

THE EVOLUTION OF EMPATHY

First let us start with the shared biological aspects of empathy. The primatologist Frans de Waal makes a compelling argument that empathy dates to prehistoric time for earlier mammalian species. Human beings seem to be hard-wired for imitation through the mirroring process, which is also seen in other primates (Iacoboni, 2009). De Waal (2009) posits that females who were attentive to their offspring—that is, they were compelled to respond in knowing ways to the needs of their young—reproduced at far greater rates than those who were distant and inattentive. He regards this attention as the foundation of care and attachment, which are threaded through our social groups. As he observes, "Every human life cycle includes stages at which we either depend on others (when we are young, old, or sick) or others depend on us (when we care for the young, old or sick). We very much rely on one another for survival" (p. 21). Attentive care requires understanding the behaviors of others, what those behaviors mean, and re-sponding appropriately. Is a baby crying because she is in pain, because she is hungry, or because she is scared? We know what those emotions feel like because we have experienced them ourselves.

Making the connection between seeing the behavior of others and under-standing what those behaviors mean requires various steps in cognitive processing. To ascertain whether the baby is crying due to pain, hunger, or something else is to move from the unconscious affective response to the more conscious processes of mentalizing, perspective-taking, and self-other awareness, which are the components of interpersonal empathy as described in chapter 1. The ability to connect with other human beings is what sup-ports survival, and our connections are best made through empathy.

There is considerable debate over what we might consider evolutionary behaviors that are biologically driven and those that are sociological be-haviors and are culturally driven, that is, learned from those around us. Em-pathy likely crosses between both of these aspects of human development. There seem to be purely biological aspects of empathy, as in mirroring, as well as psychological reasons for imitation—to foster attachment, for ex-ample, or because we are taught to behave that way. This pattern is physi-ological with cultural rationales ("don't hit your brother, that hurts; you wouldn't want him to hit you; hitting is not nice behavior, we don't do that in our family"). Although empathy may make sense from a survival stand-point, we know from history that it has not always been present among human beings. In fact, there are many historical events of genocide, torture, and slavery that point to a lack of empathy. How do we reconcile the positive aspects of empathic collaboration to promote survival with the utter absence of empathy evident in acts of war, genocide, and other human atrocities? To begin to answer that question, we need to understand the evo-lutionary and biological aspects of empathy.

Kin Selection

One of the evolutionary theories that contributes to our conceptualization of empathy is *kin selection*. Kin selection is a sociobiological explanation for *altruism*, which is related to empathy in a number of ways. Altruism is a form of concern for the welfare of others that at times can appear to be self-less and seems to be more for the benefit of the other than for oneself

(Wispé, 1978). It is considered a prosocial behavior—that is, a positive and helpful behavior within a group and on behalf of others (Batson & Shaw, 1991; Hoffman, 1981). So why would people risk their own well-being for others? Kin selection posits that the full extent of survival means that one's offspring or one's closest kin must survive, thereby passing on the genetic make-up of the parent, as well as the species (Davis, 1996; Hamilton, 1964). The connection to empathy is that altruism can be induced by the shared emotions or feelings between an observer and an observed, motivating the observer to respond (de Waal, 2008). And part of that motivation may be survival of one's kin. Simply put, over evolutionary time, those species that continued to survive most often received some nurturance and support from the previous generation. Although nurturance and support, as instinctual responses, may be biologically driven, they are typically induced through empathic triggers: a crying baby, a distress call, observation of another in pain. In the cases where the parent or caretakers did not read those empathic triggers, the offspring were more likely to die, and thus not pass on the caregiver's lack of empathic abilities (de Waal, 2009; Preston & de Waal, 2011). Or, stated in a positive way, those who drew upon empathic insight to care for young were more likely to see their offspring survive and pass on that ability. This is the foundation for kin selection.

Learned Social Behaviors

The next step from kin selection to ensure survival is to understand one's surroundings and social world well enough to be safe. This includes the ability to meet one's physiological needs, including shelter, protection from predators, and enough food for sustenance, and to differentiate between those who are friends and those who might be enemies (Carter, Harris, & Porges, 2011). Thus, "a sense of trust and sensitivity to social cues are likely elements of empathy" (Carter, Harris, & Porges, 2011, p. 179).

Because human beings cannot meet all these needs for themselves until years after birth, survival requires that there be a support network. In early human development, this network was typically a clan or tribe. The power of identification with a group and how that can promote or inhibit empathy are discussed in more detail in chapter 4. In terms of evolution, belonging to a group not only helped with survival, but also encouraged identification with others in such a way as to nurture early development of empathic

abilities. By reading others and mirroring their behaviors, we learn important tasks such as what to eat, where to sleep, and how to provide for those
resources on an ongoing basis. We also learn to read others in order to protect
ourselves from danger. Imagine living thousands of years ago, communicating with someone, and in the middle of your interactions, the expression
on your companion's face changes from engagement to surprise and fear,
and he grabs a large stick. Understanding the change in expression can save
your life, as you turn to take in what has caused your companion's sudden
change in emotion and realize you are both being observed by a wild animal.
Had you not read the other's expression correctly, you might not turn
around and even consider that there could be a danger to your life. In evolutionary terms, your inability to process the facial expressions of another
person may end with death, and the end of passing on that lack of skill.
Although this may seem like an oversimplification, imagine this happening to most human beings through history, and you can see how the ability to read situations correctly would be a dominant characteristic that is
passed on. Not only are mirroring skills and the cognitive processing of
the information important to survival of our species; so, too, are the social
skills that evolve from empathy. Looking at the evolution of our species
from a sociological perspective, Stone (2008) argues that the dual inheri-
tance theory, which treats evolution as a combination of kin selection and
learned prosocial behaviors, provides a more complete picture of human
evolution. He builds on kin selection as including a social component:
"Individuals incapable of participation in cultural cooperative groups would
have been less likely to survive and find mates" (p. 73). The unconscious
biological skills and cognitive processing abilities that underpin empathy
have aided human survival both genetically and socially.

Thus, we can argue that the evolution of empathy serves as a critical
foundation for the survival of the human species. In part empathy is biological, and in part it is learned social behavior. However, meeting the
challenge of transferring empathy beyond survival of kin to survival of the
human species has not been easy. Incidents of failure in adopting the
learned social behavioral aspects of empathy are spread throughout history.
Part of the reason for this—and it is explained in more detail in chapter 4—
is that kin selection covers only those whom we regard as kin. Race, ethnicity,
religious affiliation, and other constructs can be perceived as threats to one's
group and thus kin survival (some examples of research on this, elaborated

in chapter 4, include the impact of ingroup versus outgroup membership on feelings of empathy, as discussed in Eres & Molenberghs, 2013; Gutsell & Inzlicht, 2012; Mathur, Harad, Lipke, & Chiao, 2010; O'Brien & Ellsworth, 2012). The history of humanity is full of examples of how one group's view of the "otherness" and "foreignness" of another instigated or justified violence against it (Pinker, 2011). The perception of others, while including some biological basis such as mirroring, is heavily socially influenced. Although this makes the cognitive learned aspects of empathy malleable and hence teachable, it is also possible to be socially trained to forego empathy. But before tackling the more dynamic social aspects, it helps to understand the biological underpinnings of empathy. Although it is difficult to separate what is biological or passed on through heredity from what is social or nurtured, there are key aspects of empathy that are biological in origin.

THE BIOLOGY OF EMPATHY

From cognitive neuroscience we can see that there are brain activities that serve as foundations for empathic abilities, and we share many of these activities with other members of the animal world. Recall the mirror neuron system that was identified in chapter 1. During the 1990s, researchers in Parma, Italy, were monitoring the neurological activity in the brains of Macaque monkeys, tracking patterns in the brain that corresponded to physical actions such as grasping, holding, preparing food, and eating. One day when they took a break for lunch in the lab, they were surprised that while the animals watched the researchers eating, the monkeys' brains showed the same neural activity as if they were eating too, although they were not physically doing so (Iacoboni, 2008). The Italian researchers had discovered mirror neurons, nerve cells that in some way transmitted perceived actions as if the perceiver were doing those actions as well (Rizzolatti & Craighero, 2004). This discovery opened the door to neurological research on empathy. Based on the earlier work on monkey brain activity, coupled with breakthroughs in sophisticated brain imaging technology, scientists over the past fifteen years have been able to map observable brain activity in humans that is related to empathic actions and emotions. Although the study of empathy as a constellation of neural activities triggered by external events or images of external events that are then processed through a cognitive lens is still in its early stages, there are compelling data on just how this all works.

Empathy and Our Brain

Cognitive neuroscience has helped us to better understand empathy by identifying distinct components of it. As explained in the previous chapter, these components are both unconscious and conscious and are found in different parts of the brain. Thus, there is no definitive, single place in the brain where we can find empathy. "Recent advances in cognitive and affective neuroscience indicate that distinct but interacting brain circuits underpin the different components of empathy, each having their own developmental trajectory" (Decety, 2010, p. 266). This makes the biology of empathy rather complex. In fact, even those with expertise in understanding how the brain functions warn us that there is still a great deal to be discovered about the interactions between the systems within the brain (Bassett & Gazzaniga, 2011; Swanson, 2012). Part of the difficulty is that our ability to map the connection between the structure of the brain and all the things that it does is in the earliest of stages (Park & Friston, 2013).

So what do we know? Different regions of the brain are involved in different activities that together bring about complex behaviors such as empathy. Table 2.1 outlines brain regions that have been associated with different components and aspects of empathy, while figure 2.1 depicts some of these regions within the brain. Different parts of the brain are activated for different aspects of empathy. The articles cited for table 2.1 are just a sample of the research that has identified brain parts that are mapped to components of empathy. The most striking finding from this research is that the full scope of empathy is very complex and involves many regions and functions of the brain, all of which are activated within milliseconds of each other. It is likely that while our understanding of the brain paths for empathy has grown exponentially in recent years, there is still much that we do not understand. Consider the following explanation in this chapter to be reflective of what we know now, but keep in mind that it is still in the earliest stages of scientific confirmation. And please note that we are not neuroscientists, so admittedly this is a simplified discussion of a very complex system. Additionally, environment and upbringing affect the development of empathy in ways that are only beginning to be scientifically understood.

TABLE 2.1

EMPATHY COMPONENTS	BRAIN REGIONS ACTIVATED
Affective arousal	Amygdala (Amy)[1, 6, 8, 10, 11, 12] Orbitofrontal cortex (OFC)[1, 8, 10] hypothalamus,[8] a source of oxytocin,[2] which activates messaging for cortisol hippocampus[8] relays message to hypothalamus to turn off cortisol when levels are too high
Mirror Neuron System (MNS)	supplementary motor area (SMA)[5] anterior cingulate cortex (ACC)[5, 12] Ventral ACC[5]
Mentalizing and Theory of Mind (ToM)	ventromedial prefontal cortex (vmPFC)[1, 4, 8] temporo-parietal junction (TPJ)[4, 8, 13] bilateral superior temporal sulcus (STS)[8] dorso medial prefontal cortex (dmPFC)[4, 12]
Self-Other Awareness	medial prefontal cortex (mPFC)[1, 4, 11] ventromedial prefontal cortex (vmPFC)[8, 11] temporo-parietal junction (TPJ)[1, 13] right supramarginal gyrus (rSMG)[9]
Perspective-Taking	similar regions as ToM perigenual anterior cingulate cortex (pgACC)[6]
Emotion Regulation	anterior cingulate cortex (ACC)[3, 8, 13] medial prefontal cortex (mPFC)[1, 8, 13] ventromedial prefontal cortex (vmPFC)[8] need oxytocin[2]

Sources: 1. Decety & Michalska (2012); 2. Carter & Porges (2011); 3. Taylor (2010); 4. Koster-Hale & Saxe (2013); 5. Iacoboni (2011); 6. Lamm, Batson, & Decety (2007); 7. Kersting, Ohrmann, Pedersen, Kroker, Samberg, & Bauer (2009); 8. Decety (2010); 9. Silani, Lamm, Ruff, & Singer (2013); 10. Lamm, Silani, & Singer (2015); 11. Shamay-Tsoory (2011); 12. Eres, Decety, Louis, & Molenberghs (2015); 13. Tousignant, Eugène, & Jackson (2016).

The Brain Simplified—How Does It All Work?

The brain, a mere three pounds of spongy tissue, is extremely complex and has an incredible capacity to store and process information in ways that we are only beginning to understand (Society for Neuroscience, 2012). Basically, the brain has two functions, that of specialization and that of integration (Paus, 2011). The specialized tasks often occur in discrete regions of the brain, while the information from these tasks is shared across numerous regions in the brain. These two functions can be seen in the affective

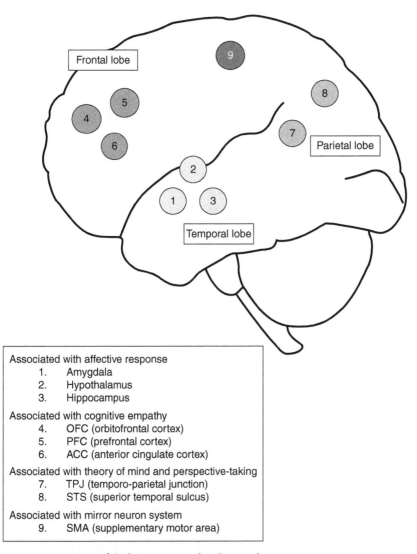

Associated with affective response
1.   Amygdala
2.   Hypothalamus
3.   Hippocampus

Associated with cognitive empathy
4.   OFC (orbitofrontal cortex)
5.   PFC (prefrontal cortex)
6.   ACC (anterior cingulate cortex)

Associated with theory of mind and perspective-taking
7.   TPJ (temporo-parietal junction)
8.   STS (superior temporal sulcus)

Associated with mirror neuron system
9.   SMA (supplementary motor area)

FIGURE 2.1 Areas of the brain associated with empathy

and cognitive aspects of empathy—stimuli are taken in through the senses after which the meaning of those stimuli are processed. The most basic responses in our brain that are related to empathy are unconscious and involve the amygdala, hypothalamus, and hippocampus, which are embedded within the center of our brain and sit on our brain stem. Together we refer to this group of brain parts as the *limbic system*. The limbic system takes in information gathered through our senses, balances it with information in our internal systems, processes all this basic input, and then sends it to other parts of the brain for more advanced cognitive processing. Specifically, the amygdala detects what is happening, the hippocampus processes it, and the hypothalamus sends out the message about it—although the steps are, in fact, more complex. For example, the amygdala is involved in three major networks of the brain, the visual system, the constellation of autonomic bodily responses, and the process of cognitive value assessments, all in a flexible way that can vary according to context (Pessoa, 2014). We rely on the limbic system to stay alive. The brain takes in information from other parts of the body such as our sense of smell or touch, how our body is feeling, such as hot or cold, as well as processing internal information such as temperature, blood balance, and hormones. Most of these inputs are detected and then directed first through the amygdala. This unconscious ability to take in external affects starts very early in life. For example, infants are able to pick up the affective states of others as demonstrated by their reactions to other infants' cries (Dondi, Simion, & Caltran, 1999; Martin & Clark, 1987).

The amygdala then coordinates responses to external stimuli, particularly those with emotional triggers. Primarily, the amygdala is concerned with stimuli that relate to fear and anxiety, probably due to our earliest needs to survive. It leaves deeper processing to other parts of the brain. The amygdala is considered the "biological relevance detector" or "central hub" that starts physical and mental responses to threats and challenges (Todd & Anderson, 2014).

The hippocampus receives input from the amygdala, processes it, and sends it to the hypothalamus (Carter & Porges, 2011; Decety, 2010). The hypothalamus regulates most unconscious body functions, such as our pulse, blood pressure, and breathing. Its overall goal is to maintain bodily equilibrium, the ideal state of survival. It responds to physical conditions including hunger, thirst, cold, warmth, and pain. It then sends out instructions to the rest of the body, directly regulating the autonomic nervous system (the processes that include blood flow, digestion, and breathing) and the pituitary gland, which in turn tells the adrenal glands to release hormones that regulate our metabolism and growth, as well as our response systems, into the blood stream. The inputs that are initially processed through our limbic system are identified in the first column of figure 1.1, in the previous chapter. Once the limbic system processes the initial inputs of stimuli there may be an immediate physical response due to mirroring of the perceived action, but then the information is also sent to the prefrontal cortex and other regions of the brain for more advanced cognitive processing. This more advanced cognitive processing includes making sense of others' actions and understanding others' motivations, which are the cognitive parts of empathy.

Imagine you are sitting and reading in a quiet room in your home. You have the afternoon all to yourself, there is no one else in the house, and you feel very relaxed. Suddenly, you hear a very loud noise. Immediately, you are startled. Your heart begins to race, and you might even have other symptoms of fright and anxiety—something unknown and out of your control has occurred, and your body is reacting physically. Senses have developed to help you understand your surroundings, especially surprises, and so now you begin that assessment process. You orient yourself in the direction from where the sound came; you pause to listen for any additional sound. Your mind begins to call on stored information: Has this ever happened before? What is in the room where the sound came from? What might make such a noise? What did the noise sound like? And in seconds you begin to formulate a theory or a plan of action. In this case, you remember that you had packed a number of boxes with books to be given away. Your memory suggests that the sound you heard might be that of a box falling. You feel confident of your theory, and when you walk into the room, you see that indeed your cognitive processing was correct: The noise came from one of the boxes that was likely off balance just enough to fall. It is also possible that you choose a different approach. Maybe instead you decide to leave and wait for help before checking out what made the noise because you heard that some homes in your neighborhood have been broken into. With this response, you are also integrating recalled information.

In this example, we are talking only about a physical stimulus of a loud noise. This demonstrates the reactions that might be involved in initiating empathy, but do not call on the additional empathic components. If we change the situation slightly so that your child is playing in that room and she screams or cries immediately after the loud sound, your cognitive processing shifts not only to trying to figure out what happened, but also to your daughter's well-being. You may also feel her surprise, fright, or pain. Your response may feel instantaneous, and it still involves affective and cognitive processing, but additional awareness comes into play. You are now activating perspective-taking, that is, what your daughter might be experiencing. These scenarios illustrate the coupling of unconscious reactions and empathic insights.

The Dual Brain Actions for Empathy

The above discussion outlines the two broad categories of brain activity that contribute to empathy—the unconscious reading of external stimuli and the processing of the sensory input through the conscious interpretation of those stimuli. Zaki and Ochsner (2013) regard this as the co-activation of *experience sharing* and *mental state attribution*. Others refer to these two processes as *affective empathy* and *cognitive empathy* (Walter, 2012) or *emotional empathy* and *cognitive empathy* (Shamay-Tsoory, 2011). Still another view distinguishes between unconscious automatic empathy and more conscious controlled empathy (Hodges & Wegner, 1997). Generally, researchers agree that these processes involve both a lower-level unconscious response that likely involves the mirror neuron system and higher order cognitive functions to determine what the stimuli and observed actions mean (Decety & Lamm, 2006; Decety & Moriguchi, 2007; Goldman, 2011; Shamay-Tsoory, 2011). Additionally, while early life neural circuitry processes affect, as humans mature, they develop the ability to interpret and understand the emotional states of others (Decety, 2010).

We understand empathy to be a coming together of multiple components, both unconscious and conscious. Furthermore, we consider the practice of bringing the unconscious to a level of consciousness as one that can be developed and taught. In chapter 1, we outlined the five components that we regard as being basic to interpersonal empathy, and the two additional components that relate to social empathy. These components have been subject to neuroscience research (Decety, 2011, 2015; Decety & Lamm, 2006; Decety & Moriguchi, 2007), which has found that "although both emotional and cognitive components of empathy may operate partly autonomously, it is likely that every empathic response will evoke both components to some extent, depending on the social context" (Shamay-Tsoory, 2011, p. 22). This is the entire rationale for this book—to identify and define the components that together make up the full scope of empathy and to then understand how those components fit together in response to one's social, historical, and personal contexts.

WHAT IS THE RATIONALE FOR THESE COMPONENTS?

By now you may be struck by the numerous terms that are used in relation to empathy and the seeming interchangeability of those terms. This makes a standard definition of empathy difficult to come by and renders what one means when using the term somewhat unclear (Gerdes, Segal, & Lietz, 2010). Our focus on components, five for interpersonal empathy that combine with two additional components to describe social empathy, is grounded in years of research and professional experience. In chapter 1, we presented and described these seven components. Here we will review those descriptions and place the actions of each component in relation to the brain activities that correspond with feeling empathic. The following descriptions are based on physically healthy brains, unless so noted.

Looking at the components from a neurological perspective also helps us to see how they fit together and operate as a whole. As stated previously, activation of all the components leads to the full scope of empathy. However, having weaker applications of some of the components does not necessarily mean a person is not empathic. We see the components as ways to break empathy into understandable parts that can be highlighted for greater development or understanding across different people. Each component becomes a tool of empathy, which when operating together allows for the full impact of empathy.

Affective Response

Physically reacting unconsciously to an observed action is affective response. Our unconsciously mimicking actions that we see or imagine is typically the first step in developing an empathic response (Iacoboni, 2008) and is initially processed through the limbic system. If we see someone trip and fall, we may well have a physical sensation of falling ourselves, that is, of matching or mirroring the actions we see. The sharing of the behavior is automatic and actually stimulates the same region of our brains that would be stimulated if we were actually having the same physical experience

(Iacoboni, 2008; Preston & de Wall, 2002). For example, in patients with lesions on the part of the brain that is a sensory area (the anterior insular cortex), their ability to ascertain pain in others was slower than of others without such a deficit or even those with deficits in another brain region (Gu et al., 2012). This research suggests that damage to the affective response area of the brain, while not necessarily stopping empathic feelings altogether, results in slower, more deliberate reasoning as opposed to a faster intuitive response.

The affective initial trigger is believed to help us focus on or tune in to another person and begins the process of understanding the actions of others. The unconscious physiological sensation certainly is a way to get our attention. This is the starting point for experiencing empathy, but alone it is not empathy. The next step is grasping the intention behind or the meaning of the observed actions. Gallese (2007) sees the mirror neuron system (MNS) as being part of a process that involves embodied simulation, which operates on a neural level: The body draws on its own experiential knowledge of having lived experiences that reflect or match the physical sensation. We see this process as moving to the second component, affective mentalizing, the bridge between unconscious affective response and cognitive processing.

Affective Mentalizing

Not only does experiencing an unconscious physiological affective response trigger a mirrored physical sensation; so too does imagining having the experience of the same observed action. This is the start of cognitive processing, a bridge between the purely affective unconscious neural response to external stimuli, on the one hand, to cognitive processing of the meaning of the observed actions, on the other. Neurologically, when our brain is stimulated by observing the actions of another, as if we were experiencing the same actions, images may develop and enter our consciousness, initiating the process of mentalizing the affective response. Research has found that this response can also arise without physically viewing an action take place. Exposure to a narrative description of an action, along with visual cues about it, can actually activate the limbic system as well as the neocortical regions of the brain (Schnell, Bluschke, Konradt, & Walter, 2011). Thus, when hearing or reading a story, we visualize the actions in our minds, which then triggers the MNS giving us the physical sensation of doing the action. It is important to note that mentalizing alone, or inferring about the mental state of others based on affect, is not enough for empathy. Mentalizing does not involve the emotional aspect of stepping into the situation of another (Singer & Decety, 2011). That process involves the next two components, self-other awareness and perspective-taking.

However, insofar as affective mentalizing forms a bridge between un-conscious and conscious processing, it is the pathway to social living. It allows us to go beyond unconscious reactions to participate in a complex emotional system with others (Winkielman, Berridge & Sher, 2011). We can care about others and have others care about us in context-specific ways. In terms of one of today's cultural memes, it is our conscious processing of events around us that makes us human beings and not zombies.

Self-Other Awareness

Self-awareness, understanding how we interact with others, is character-ized by understanding ourselves through the passage of time—we have a past, a present, and a future (Keenan, Oh, & Amati, 2011). The prefrontal cortex plays a key role in the ways that we are self-aware (Morin, 2004). For example, we can recognize images of ourselves, and know that we are dis-tinct from others, and this realization is a form of self-awareness. Once we have the ability to recognize ourselves as distinct from others, then we need to understand ourselves as different from others. "The prerequisite for social communication, including the experiences of empathy, is that the two agents can preserve their individuality" (Decety & Lamm, 2006, p. 1153). Neurologically, we can see separate brain activity for self-processing and other processing, as well as overlapping activity (Decety & Sommerville, 2003). This ability is reflected in interactions of processes distributed throughout the brain, particularly in the prefrontal cortex and the infe-rior parietal lobule, as opposed to being located in a specific brain region (Decety & Moriguchi, 2007). Although self-awareness is important to one's survival, without other-awareness we are prone to projecting our thinking onto that of another. Projection is not empathy because it is egocentric and does not assess whether the other person is indeed feeling or think-ing that way. Essentially, "empathy requires making a link between the self and other, but without confusing the self and other" (Decety & Hodges,

2006, p. 103). Thus, in order to fully develop self-other awareness, we need to develop the next component, perspective-taking.

Perspective-Taking

Recall from chapter 1 that perspective-taking involves "the mental flexibility to intentionally adopt the perspective of the other" (Decety, 2005, p. 144), or in colloquial terms, "walking in someone else's shoes." It is often linked to Theory of Mind (ToM), which was also discussed in chapter 1. The ability to step into the mind of someone else is very complicated. It requires synthesizing several inputs: what we see about another person, what we think about the person's actions, what those actions mean to us, and what those actions mean to the other person. This complexity is matched in the neural action accompanying perspective-taking. The tasks of perspective-taking and ToM involve at least four major brain regions, the prefrontal cortex, the cingulate cortex, and the left and right temporo-parietal junctions (Saxe, 2006). This is not surprising, given the complexity of putting yourself into the experience of another and figuring out what that person is thinking.

Perspective-taking develops later in human development than affective response and self-other awareness, likely because it draws on executive functions of the prefrontal cortex, which also develop later (Decety & Lamm, 2006). This longer period of development, or maturation, may be because in order to take the perspective of another person, we need to know ourselves and set aside our own interpretations. Empathy involves a balancing act between self-awareness and taking the perspective of someone else. "An essential aspect of empathy is to recognize the other person as like the self, while maintaining a clear separation between the self and other" (Decety & Moriguchi, 2007, p. 31). It seems that we are fundamentally egocentric (possibly the default for survival) and thus must develop *mental flexibility* to toggle between our own perspective and that of another (Decety, Jackson, & Brunet, 2007).

Perspective-taking is much more difficult than it may seem. People may think about what it might be like for them to be in the situation of others, but this often is not an empathic way of perspective-taking. Coplan (2011) makes the distinction between *self-oriented* perspective-taking as opposed to *other-oriented* perspective-taking. The difference is imagining that "I am you in your situation" (other-oriented) as opposed to "I am me in your situation" (self-oriented). Being other-oriented in your perspective-taking means putting yourself entirely in the position of another, letting go of how you might react, and instead imagining how the other person might react. Neurologically, brain neuron activity differs when imagining our own pain as opposed to imagining another's pain (Jackson, Brunet, Meltzoff, & Decety, 2006). Such a neurological difference may reflect the active understanding of feeling what another is feeling, but not owning it as one's own, the hallmark of perspective-taking. Recent research supports this ever so slight variation in neural activity in self-pain and that of another. The neural system for the sharing of pain may be broader and reflect not just the overlap of neural circuits, but the "coordinated activity" of networks. The process requires complex tasks including neurological circuits and brain networks, and may even be influenced by social variables (Betti & Aglioti, 2016).

In addition to the tendency to be self-oriented, another obstacle to perspective-taking is *correspondence bias*. Correspondence bias is the tendency for people to interpret behavior based on perceived personality traits rather than the situation or context (Howell & Shepperd, 2011). In other words, what a person does corresponds to who we think that person is. For example, we see someone trip and assume the person is clumsy rather than notice that there is a gap in the sidewalk, or on a more global level, we see people of another race who are poor and assume it is a function of their race and not the context in which they live. This global aspect is addressed under the contextual understanding component of social empathy. Correspondence bias on a personal level is related to our limited understanding of the power of a given situation, which leads us to underestimate or overestimate it and have unrealistic expectations about how others should behave under the circumstances (Gilbert & Malone, 1995).

The process of taking in the experiences of others and making meaning of it can be overwhelming. Consider observing the physical pain of someone you visit in the hospital or the emotional pain of someone who has just experienced the death of a parent, or on a positive note, the joy of a friend getting a new job after months of unemployment. These are strong emotions to process empathically. In order to step into their shoes, we need to keep our own emotions in check. If we do not, we lose track of the other person, and become consumed with our own feelings. This is where the role of emotion regulation, the next component, comes into play.

Emotion Regulation

In order to experience the full scope of empathy, we have to be able to deal with our own emotions. Emotion regulation refers to one's ability to manage or modulate the intensity, duration, direction (positive or negative), or form of one's emotions (Cole, Martin & Dennis, 2004; Eisenberg, Smith, Sadovsky, & Spinrad, 2004). The brain regions associated with emotion regulation include those associated with the other components of empathy— namely, the prefrontal cortex, the anterior cingulate cortex, the amygdala, and the hippocampus (Decety, Jackson, & Brunet, 2007). The involvement of multiple brain regions reflects the complex nature of emotion regulation, which requires modulating both the emotions that arise somatically from unconscious affective responses and the feelings that accompany taking the perspective of others. Like development of the cognitive regions of the brain, development of emotion regulation occurs during childhood and adolescence, and when successfully done, helps people cope with stress throughout their lives (Silvers, Buhle & Ochsner, 2014).

Without the ability to manage our own feelings, we would forget that there is another person and feel their emotions as if they are our own. This is often referred to as *emotional contagion*, which is not empathy because there is no awareness of the other or of the fact that the emotions are brought about by observing another person (Singer & Decety, 2011). For example, mob behavior, or being "swept up in the crowd," can be the result of emotional contagion.

The ability to monitor one's emotions also plays a significant role in social relations. Research on children has found evidence that having a high level of effortful control or the ability to modulate one's behavior at will, which is central to emotion regulation, is related to prosocial behavior while those children who lack that ability are at greater risk for behavioral and emotional problems (Eisenberg, Smith, Sadovsky & Spinrad, 2004). Not only is emotion regulation good for social interactions, it also seems to be linked to our quality of life. In research involving adolescents, those engaging in healthy modes of emotion regulation reported a better quality of life (Phillips & Power, 2007).

Although we include emotion regulation as a key component of empathy, in many ways it is a facilitator of all the other components of empathy. Without the ability to manage our feelings, each aspect of empathy would be difficult to experience. Think back to the example earlier in this chapter about the sudden loud noise resulting in elevated heart rate and fear. In order to begin the process of cognitively figuring out what is happening, one has to calm down enough to think through what might have caused the loud noise. That is emotion regulation. When sharing time with a friend who is grieving and finding ourselves sharing the grief while saying things that are supportive, that is emotion regulation. And even watching an exciting movie that has us sitting on the edge of our seat requires emotion regulation so we can enjoy watching the show.

PUTTING IT ALL TOGETHER

With these five components operating effectively, we can experience full empathic feelings for others. It is also helpful to think of empathy on a continuum in terms of both the extent to which we can engage in each component fully and the extent to which we can engage all five for each situation we encounter. We still need to better understand how empathy varies across cultures, by social conditions, and what might inhibit or amplify empathy (Hollan, 2012). Empathy is contextual, and even for the same person the intensity of empathic insight can vary on any given day or in different situations. Think about how hard it is to feel someone else's sadness when you are sad yourself. You might be spending so much energy on regulating your emotions so that your own sadness does not paralyze you that you cannot also process another person's sadness. Or consider when you are in a great mood and do not want to hear about someone else's trouble; here you are may be guarding against emotions that might be aroused if you engage with someone else. Even being tired may impact how effectively we regulate our emotions or how accurately we interpret the experiences of others. Because there are so many competing emotions and the energy needed to process those emotions is not unlimited, we may curb our empathic feelings (sometimes consciously, sometimes unconsciously). And because affective mentalizing, self-other awareness, perspective-taking, and emotion regulation are cognitively developed abilities, it may take years and conscious effort to fully develop them. Thus, knowledge about the components gives us a framework for seeing how empathy develops and can be built, with an awareness that it is an ongoing process that can vary across settings. We can train ourselves and others to become more attuned empathically, component by component. Our experience is that the more we can enhance each component, the more we can develop as empathic individuals.

BROADER APPLICATION OF THE COMPONENTS: SOCIAL EMPATHY

Expanding our empathic insights to broader social situations is challenging. How do we understand the experiences of individuals and groups who are different from us, often living in places we have never visited? We already know that we have a tendency toward correspondence bias—that is toward seeing the behaviors of others as a function of their personalities or traits while ignoring the situational aspects (Gilbert & Malone, 1995). In addition, we have other biases such as deeper empathic tendencies for those who are similar to us over those who are perceived as different from us. In chapter 4 we provide a more extensive discussion of these tendencies.

The challenge is to be more expansive in empathic insight, which we can do by incorporating social empathy in our thinking. Social empathy is the ability to understand people from other groups by perceiving or experiencing their life situations and as a result gaining insight into the social structures that may contribute to differences, particularly disparities and inequalities, in social conditions (Segal, 2011, 2014). The goal of social empathy is to serve as a tool to better understand those whom we see as different from us and with whom we do not share experiences and identities. We become more socially empathic through application of two additional components, contextual understanding and macro self-other awareness/perspective-taking. Based on the interpersonal components of empathy, these components include a dimension of social justice, such that we can address the structural disparities that we discover through empathic insight (Segal & Wagaman, in press).

Contextual Understanding

One of the limits of empathy comes from a barrier or an inability to fully assess a given context (Singer & Lamm, 2009). A leading researcher on the neuroscience of empathy, Jean Decety, agrees that social context is important: "The roots of empathy are subsumed in the evolution of parental care and group living, which explains why empathy is influenced by social context, especially group membership" (Decety, 2015, p. 4).

For those in helping professions who use empathic insights in their work, understanding the lived experiences and contexts of those with whom they work is vital: "If therapists are to be maximally empathic, it is important for them to have a sense of their clients' current and past contexts and life histories in order to build an adequate understanding of what is emotionally significant for them and to gain an understanding of what motivates their actions" (Watson & Greenberg, 2011, p. 130).

Neurologically, therapeutically, and hence cognitively, context matters. In a brain imaging study that coded the activity of the MNS, participants were shown one of two settings with videos of three difference conditions: context, action, and intention (Iacoboni et al., 2005). In one setting, the context was a table with a teapot, a teacup, a plate of cookies, and containers of sugar and cream, suggesting a tea party was to take place; in the second setting, the context was a messy table with the same items, but used and with crumbs scattered about. The action videos were one of a hand grasping a tea cup with no context, a second of the hand grasping the teacup from the unused table and a third video of the hand grasping the teacup from the messy table. The goal was to see if the MNS activity differed by context, rather than simply by actions. The researchers found that "observing grasping actions embedded in contexts yielded greater activity in mirror neuron areas in the inferior frontal cortex than observing grasping actions in the absence of contexts or while observing contexts only" (p. 530). Our brain differentiates between the grasp of a teacup to enable drinking at a tea party and the grasp of a teacup to clean up afterwards. The same physical action is understood differently given the different contexts.

Walter (2012) presents the concepts of a "low and high road to empathy," with the low road being the affective response and the high road using higher cognitive processes. Although this is similar to the dual brain actions discussed in the section on interpersonal empathy, he argues that the higher cognitive processes should include information about context and the situations of others for the full extent of empathy to be manifest.

The tea cup experiment and Walter's insistence that higher levels of empathy include information about context stress the importance of integrating contextual understanding to gain full empathic insight. Contextual understanding is even more crucial in terms of greater group differences. In order to understand those who are significantly different from ourselves, we must take into account the historical and social contexts within which the targets of our empathy live. Understanding context includes analyzing history and social structures within which groups function. This is the first step in gaining socially empathic awareness. The next component is built on contextual understanding.

Macro Self-Other Awareness/Perspective-Taking

We already know how important self-other awareness and perspective-taking are to the full scope of interpersonal empathy. These skills are also important for empathic insight on a broader level so that we can understand other cultures and groups who differ from our own. The reason for linking both interpersonal skills is that in the macro context, the differences between groups is a priori, it is why we need to engage in macro perspective-taking. The two skills are intertwined on the macro level. Applying self-other awareness and perspective-taking more broadly and in relation to the environments of others moves us from interpersonal empathy to social empathy.

For example, the importance of broader perspective-taking when interacting with other cultures has been recognized by the United States Army in recent years. In order to better train U.S. soldiers, the Army developed training in what they call "social perspective-taking" as a way to assess local cultures and populations (Roan et al., 2009). The emphasis is on soldiers understanding the historical, social, and cultural features of countries in which they are stationed so that they will better understand the perspective of the local inhabitants. This is application of the macro self-other awareness/perspective-taking component, while considering the context.

The brain regions associated with macro perspective-taking are similar to those involved in general perspective-taking (prefrontal cortical areas). However, the extent of neural activation and the patterns can differ depending on the degree of familiarity or comfort with the target of observation (Gutsell & Inzlicht, 2012; Lamm, Meltzoff, & Decety, 2009; Mathur, Harada, Lipke & Chiao, 2010). This means that using our abilities for perspective-taking and keeping track of our self-awareness in relation to others when we are interpreting the lives of people who are different from us requires additional cognitive skills and training. Interpersonal and social empathy are related (more on this in chapter 5), but processing on one level of empathy does not necessarily mean processing on the other. Although we are hard-wired for unconscious affective responses and have the MNS that helps us mimic others and might even help us differentiate contexts, both interpersonal and social empathy have cognitive aspects that must be learned.

The benefits of empathy between individuals are similar to those of empathy between groups. Applying empathic perspective-taking to other groups can improve intergroup relations (Eisenberg, Eggum, & Di Gunta, 2010). When perspective-taking is done through increasing self-other overlap (sharing representations of the self and the other in our minds, or putting ourselves in the place of others and vice versa), we can increase social bonds by decreasing prejudice and stereotyping (Galinsky, Ku, & Wang, 2005). Even going through the exercise of imagining the perspective and experience of others who are different without actually experiencing it first-hand can motivate positive social change (Turner & Crisp, 2010; Vezzali, Capozza, Stathi & Giovannini, 2012). Thus, macro thinking about other groups and imagining what it would be like to live in their situations can be a powerful tool to enhance empathy on a broader social level.

With social empathy, we build on the interpersonal empathic skills we use on a person-to-person level and apply those abilities to a broader context. This broader application helps us to gain insight into other groups and cultures, as well as gaining insight leads to broader empathy, both of which can lead to action to change social structures to reflect greater social justice. The relationship between interpersonal and social empathy is explored in more detail in chapter 5 where we share findings from research we conducted on this topic.

OTHER NEUROSCIENCE ISSUES RELATED TO EMPATHY

There are newly emerging research areas of neuroscience that relate to empathy. Researchers have begun to consider how genetics and neurochemical pathways are involved in empathy. Research on the neuropeptide *oxytocin* (OXT) links this neural transmitter (hormone) to empathy, group participation, social cooperation, reciprocity of trust, and reduction of social stress reactivity (De Dreu & Kret, 2016; Heinrichs, Chen & Domes, 2013). It seems to do all these things through lowering cortisol levels and hence stress levels, and it is involved in dampening fear and modulating emotions. Because OXT can be administered rather easily, primarily through nasal spray, its relationship to prosocial behavior and a greater sense of well-being is of great interest. It could be a way to enhance empathy and treat symptoms of depression, anxiety, and other psychiatric disorders (Mayo Clinic, 2014). However, although the association between OXT and prosocial behavior has been neurologically observed, the biological mechanism of how this works is largely unknown (Uzefovsky et al., 2015). OXT may be a messenger of empathy that already exists in people in various levels, but may have no effect on building empathy. We might find that enhancing empathic abilities increases OXT, or that increasing OXT through interventions can increase empathy. Maybe prescribing OXT can provide a faster biological way of increasing empathy, which in turn might improve social well-being. However, OXT is part of a large array of brain chemicals involved in transmitting information on social functioning, so it is likely to be a long time before researchers can clearly articulate how OXT is involved in empathy.

Another area of neuroscience that may have a significant impact on empathy is stress. Robert Sapolsky, a biologist and neurologist who has conducted a great deal of research on the impact of long-term stress on our physical and mental health (2004), has extensively analyzed the process whereby our body recognizes and deals with threats to our survival, or perceived threats to our survival. He argues that the body is well developed for these occasional or periodic threats. However, today we are beset by chronic stress—worries about money, jobs, family, relationships; we also experience prolonged stress, as in the case of military personnel serving in times of war or growing up in a violent home. The problem is that while our body can handle stressful events, it has not developed the mechanisms to deal with prolonged stress:

> For the vast majority of beasts on this planet, stress is about a short-term crisis, after which it's either over with or you're over with. When we sit around and worry about stressful things, we turn on the same physiological responses—but they are potentially a disaster when provoked chronically. A large body of evidence suggests that stress-related disease emerges, predominantly, out of the fact that we so often activate a physiological system that has evolved for responding to acute physical emergencies, but we turn it on for months on end, worrying about mortgages, relationships, and promotions. (p. 6)

This is important in a discussion of overall well-being, but you may be asking what does this have to do with empathy? Many of the brain regions involved in empathy, including the amygdala, the hippocampus, and especially the prefrontal cortex, are affected by prolonged stress (Arnsten, 2009; Lupien, McEwen, Gunnar, & Heim, 2009). Besides compromising these brain functions, prolonged stress can also lead to poor physical health outcomes such as high blood pressure, obesity, depression, anxiety, and a depressed immune system (Sapolsky, 2004; Taylor, 2010), which may damage the neural pathways needed to fully process all the components of empathy. Long-term stress diminishes the ability for emotion regulation (Evans & Fuller-Roswell, 2013; Kim & Cicchetti, 2009) which we know to be a key component of empathy. According to the National Scientific Council on the Developing Child (2014), "When children experience toxic stress [ongoing, long-term], their cortisol levels remain elevated for prolonged periods of time. Both animal and human studies show that long-term elevations in cortisol levels can alter the function of a number of neural systems, suppress the immune response, and even change the architecture of regions of the brain that are essential for learning and memory" (p. 3).

A review of studies on structural brain changes associated with childhood maltreatment found that there was repeated evidence of functional abnormalities in the prefrontal cortex, the orbitofrontal cortex, the hippocampus, and the amygdala and that the extent of abnormalities correlated with age of onset and duration of maltreatment (Fawley-King & Merz, 2014).

These regions of the brain are all critical to the development of empathy. Future neuroscience research is needed to map the relationship between empathy in the brain and the impact of stress. For now we know enough to be concerned that environmental events that compromise the health of our brains may also compromise our ability to be empathic. Although this may paint a bleak picture for those who grow up in stressful environments, we also know that the brain is malleable and can be changed. In chapter 4 we discuss this property in more detail.

PUTTING IT ALL TOGETHER II

By pulling together all the components of interpersonal and social empathy, we can experience the full scope of empathy. Although there may not be a linear flow from component to component, there is a physiological and cognitive order that when fully developed helps us make sense of our observations and emotions. We are constantly unconsciously assessing our surroundings and the behavior of others. It is likely that we first sense things in a visceral way—our brain mirrors actions we see or hear about. That mirroring process puts us in the place of others, and invites cognitive processing of what those affective feelings might mean. If we have developed a good sense of our own identity and the mental flexibility to step into the experiences of others without losing our separate sense of self, then we are well on our way to making empathic interpretations. We can best do so if we monitor our own emotional equilibrium—that is, we feel the emotions of others while recognizing that the origins of these emotions belong to someone else. We keep our own emotions in check, and consequently are fully able to analyze what the other person may be feeling and thinking. Of course we are not always right, but at least we are poised to interact in ways that can lead to verification of our interpretations. Having a concerned look on your face when someone is crying is a good way to lead into asking how the other person is feeling, or even directly asking why the person is crying. Matching the emotions of others makes people feel understood and connected. We are acting *with* the other, and that creates a social bond. When we do this on a broader level in order to interpret the lived experiences of other groups or cultures, we raise our empathic awareness to include social, political, and cultural interpretations of what life is like for those others. This can lead to empathy on a global level, which may sound unrealistic, but given our technological connections all across the world, it is certainly possible. Thus, each component, which can be learned and developed, is a piece of the puzzle we call empathy. Our challenge is to put them all together so that we can experience the full effect of being empathic in all aspects of our lives. And the benefits of being empathic are significant, as discussed more fully in the next chapter.

Why Is Empathy Important?

WHEN WE HEAR THE WORD EMPATHY, most of us think of something good, that is, a positive way to treat other people. We have already touched on altruism and prosocial behaviors in connection with empathy, and for most of us, empathy does suggest a positive social trait that is connected to giving and caring behaviors. But just saying so is not enough. How is empathy related to positive actions? In this chapter we explore how empathy connects to positive human attributes and actions, why empathy is such an important part of human relationships and social living, and the role of empathy in social relations.

BEYOND BIOLOGY AND SURVIVAL

First let's return to biology and the primatologist Frans de Waal. Primates are social animals, and as such need to cooperate for survival. Based on numerous experiments and observations, de Waal (2012) has noted the "importance of mammalian prosocial tendencies" and indicated that the "full spectrum of empathy-based altruism" can be found among nonhuman primates and extends to humans (p. 875). Although de Waal warns that prosocial responses are biased toward those who are part of our groups (for both primates and humans) and likely evolved for survival of those groups, these behaviors can also be "emancipated" from the original evolutionary purpose to extend prosocial behavior and altruism to other groups for reasons that go beyond survival. In this way, he sees behaviors that help others, without necessarily helping the giver, to be freed from the biology of kin selection. We can have empathic feelings beyond kin, although it requires the work of cognitive processing to do so. Thus, empathy goes beyond biology.

Others argue that culturally transmitted traits may be just as strong as biological imperatives in terms of developing and passing on prosocial behaviors. Bell, Richerson, and McElreath (2009) take a cultural anthropological perspective on the transmission of prosocial behavior and altruism. Using data on world values and genetics within and between fifty-nine pairs of neighboring countries, they found more support for cultural group selection to transmit social values than they did for genetic group selection. They interpret these findings to suggest that cultural rules that mandated cooperation evolved over time and consequently exerted pressure for the selection of those who fit the social structure, that is, those who demonstrated prosocial cooperative behaviors. It is not hard to imagine that in tight clans or tribes, there would be a certain amount of exclusion of those whose behavior was contrary to the best interests of the group. The thinking is that those who exhibited antisocial behaviors would be less likely to marry and more likely to be banished, while those who behaved in cooperative and prosocial ways would be favored and hence pass on those traits genetically and culturally to future offspring. They refer to this as *gene-culture coevolution*.

The ability to express and share emotions through verbal communication also has a biological basis. Humans are the only species that can put into words how they are feeling, what they are feeling, and why (Harris, 2000). This unique biological ability contributes greatly to the cultural transmission of prosocial behaviors. Through words we can instruct children on how to behave, and we can teach them to express their emotions. With conversation we can also confirm if what the other person is feeling is what we think the other is feeling. This vocalized confirmation is not available to other species. So whether we are prosocial for biological or cultural reasons, we are uniquely positioned to be learners of social behavior through both means of transmission, with special abilities for the cultural learning of prosocial behaviors.

The combination of biological proclivity towards positive social interactions and learned cultural support for such behaviors fits the composition of empathy. When people are behaving in a prosocial manner, the biological drives of mirroring and affective response are acted upon through cognitive processing. Thus, empathy, as a form of prosocial behavior, is also likely a product of gene-culture coevolution or the combination of biological and cultural transmission. And consequently, empathy has helped human beings develop and prosper as a species.

THE POSITIVE ASPECTS OF EMPATHY

How has empathy extended beyond its role in evolutionary survival? Empathy is found in a number of human interactions, including altruistic, cooperative, and attachment behaviors. These ways to interact are considered positive contributions to our social living, and thus reinforce the importance of empathy. Each of these aspects and its relationship to empathy is worthy of a deeper look so that we can understand the full scope of empathic actions, as well as recognize those behaviors that are truly empathic.

Prosocial Behavior

Like the term *empathy*, the term *prosocial* has broad and various meanings. We consider *prosocial behavior* to be an umbrella term for a number of positive social behaviors that include altruism, cooperation, and attachment. Generally, it can be defined as voluntary actions that benefit other people or society (Eisenberg, 1986). Overall, research has shown that empathy is important for the development of prosocial behaviors. However, prosocial behavior can be the result of numerous factors besides empathy, including guilt or moral principle, desire for personal gain or social recognition, or even emotional relief, as when uncomfortable feelings arise from a distressing situation, and we take action to improve that situation to help ourselves feel better (Eisenberg, Eggum, & Di Giunta, 2010). If we are on the receiving end of a prosocial behavior, that is, when someone is being caring, thoughtful, supportive, or helping, we may not be all that concerned with why. However, understanding the why of prosocial behaviors can help us to learn how to be prosocial and how to activate prosocial behaviors in others.

One of the key pieces to empathy, mirroring, may be directly linked to prosocial behavior. Research has found that imitation increases prosocial behavior (van Baaren, Holland, Kawakami, & van Knippenberg, 2004). As described in chapter 1, in a study that involved asking random passersby for directions to a train station that was a fifteen- to twenty-minute walk away, when the researcher mirrored their posture, facial expressions, and speech, the passersby were more inclined to accompany the researcher to the train station than they were if they were not mimicked (Müller, Maaskant, van Baaren, & Dijksterhuis, 2012). The researchers concluded that "mimicry not only makes people more helpful when it comes to small favors, but also allows them to ignore the substantial costs possibly involved in helping others" (p. 896). In addition, when we are copied by others, we can feel noticed and respected, adding to the power of mimicry (van Baaren, Janssen, Chartrand, & Dijksterhuis, 2009).

We know that imitation is a component of empathy in that it involves unconscious affective responses and the MNS (van Baaren, Janssen, Chartrand, & Dijksterhuis, 2009). Thus, the link between empathy and acting in a prosocial manner is likely to be at least partially neurologically connected.

In addition to being linked to empathy, prosocial behavior has a reciprocal bonus. Research on building prosocial behavior among children found that doing good for others can also promote personal well-being and acceptance by peers (Layous, Nelson, Oberle, Schonert-Reichl, & Lyubomirsky, 2012). Being a "good person" may indeed help others to like and accept you. This connection may also be true for empathy, such that the more empathic we are with others, the more they connect with us and have positive feelings for us. Engaging in prosocial behaviors also helps people who have experienced loss or trauma make meaning out of the challenges they face and promoting the process of developing resilience (Lietz, 2011).

Although there is strong agreement that empathy is related to prosocial behaviors, there may be a limit to this connection when the target of concern is more distant. Analyzing social survey data that included self-reports on measures of fifteen prosocial behaviors and a measure of empathic concern, Einolf (2008) found that most of the behaviors were correlated with empathy, but that the strongest were found for those behaviors that involved informal helping and the person needing help was directly present. There were less significant correlations with more distant prosocial behaviors such as volunteering, charitable giving, and donating blood. These findings suggest that the power of personal mimicry or some other form of personal connection strengthens the likelihood of engaging in prosocial behaviors. We will explore in the next chapter the power of personal connection and group similarities on empathic feelings.

Altruism

Altruistic behaviors are typically considered a type of prosocial behavior (Eisenberg, 1986). Early definitions suggested that altruistic behavior is "directed to the well-being of another person or group and must involve at least some nontrivial self-sacrifice" (Wispé, 1978, p. 305). The uniqueness of altruism is that it is motivated by concerns about others in a way that is not motivated by personal or practical considerations. That is not to say that altruistic actions cannot result in personal gain—a good deed can elicit public recognition or a reward—but that is not the underlying motivation. One of the difficulties in clearly identifying altruistic behavior that is other-focused is that rarely are human beings that single-minded in their relations with others. In other words, in a situation where I might step up to help someone, I might say that my only concern is for the well-being of another person, but secretly I may be hoping to be noticed for such a gallant act. Saying we do something good for external recognition feels very egotistical, so we often do not let that part of the motivation come out publicly.

The debate regarding motivations for altruistic actions has been going on for years (Hoffman, 1981). Almost three decades ago, experimental psychologist C. Daniel Batson (1991) conducted numerous research studies to examine how empathy, sympathy, and personal distress lead people to engage in helping behaviors. At the time, the prevailing belief was that helping others was motivated by expectation of gaining of some personal benefit. Yes, prosocial behaviors might be helpful to others, but the dominant force behind instances of altruism was ego-centered. Batson and colleagues reviewed and conducted numerous experiments to explore the possibility that people are altruistic for the sake of helping others, without being motivated by personal gain. Finding that selfless action can be inspired by empathy, he proposed an *empathy-altruism hypothesis* (Batson & Shaw, 1991; Batson et al., 1991). After decades of further research, Batson (2012; Batson, Lishner, & Stocks, 2015) concluded that the hypothesis is correct—that empathic concern can indeed produce true altruistic motivation, that is, motivation that is based on the other, not the self: "Empathic concern—other-oriented emotion elicited by and congruent with the perceived welfare of another in need—produces altruistic motivation—motivation with the ultimate goal of increasing the other's welfare by removing the need"

(Batson, 2012, p. 50). While Batson does agree that knowing all of a person's motivations may be impossible, enough controlled experiments have been conducted in which people have acted on behalf of others to show that they did so without personal gain, and in some cases with considerable cost. Davis (1996) concedes that empathy may be the motivation behind truly selfless acts, but that we may never know, given the complexity of people's thinking. He points to the possibility that guilt for not taking action or a deeply held sense of moral duty may be part of the motivation.

These links between empathy and altruism are based on theories and research that predated the confirmation of the neurological components of empathy and the role of mirror neurons in instigating the empathic process. What we know today about our unconscious affective responses due to mirroring and mentalizing, along with our cognitive processing of those stimuli through perspective-taking, self-other awareness, and emotion regulation does not rule out the possibility of acting out of empathic concern solely for the benefit of another. But de Waal (2008) argues that it is futile to try to separate the self from the altruistic behavior and that maybe there is no reason to do so. "The beauty of the empathy-altruism connection [is that] it gives individuals an emotional stake in the welfare of others" (p. 292). That seems to be its power, too: we become engaged in the life of others through empathy, and are there to respond whether or not our doing so is beneficial to ourselves.

One word of caution about the empathy-altruism connection. Most of the research looks at empathic concern, which takes a more narrow view than the full scope of empathy. The definition of empathic concern invokes sympathy, compassion, and tender feelings for another, especially when that person is in distress (Batson & Shaw, 1991). That does not include perspective-taking (Batson, 2012), which today is considered a key component of empathy. It also does not include emotion regulation, which we regard as another key component of empathy.

For example, a therapist may be empathic with a client who is struggling with addiction, but for therapeutic reasons may not engage in sympathy— that is, overtly sharing the client's pain—because the client needs to feel the therapist is in control and not party to the client's addiction. Likewise healthcare providers who are exposed constantly to patients' pain or distress need to balance their empathic response, that is, not become so affected by empathic sharing that serving in their professional capacity can be compromised. Decety (2012) warns that the empathic response to patients in distress can be problematic: caring about the other can lead to helping, but it can also lead to high levels of distress on the part of the caregiver, which, in turn, can interfere with providing good care. "It is crucial that health professionals develop regulatory mechanisms to dampen the emotional response to suffering patients just enough to avoid the collateral damage that comes from caring excessively (e.g., compassion fatigue), yet not to the extent that they become blunted or insensitive to the affective signal expressed by patients" (p. 255).

These are very difficult lines to draw, and that is where emotion regulation comes into play. The full scope of empathy includes more than concern, and may or may not result in altruistic behavior. Another way to view this is that altruism is a subset of empathy, but empathy does not always involve altruism. Instead, altruism is one of several possible empathic responses to others.

Morality and Justice

In the previous section, we mentioned that moral principles might be motivation for taking action on behalf of others. Morality refers to judgment of what is considered right and wrong and whether behaviors are regarded as right or wrong (Young & Waytz, 2013). It is concerned with knowing the difference between goodness and badness, and acting accordingly. This ability supports social life. For example, a moral precept stipulated by religious doctrine, such as "thou shalt not kill," is now codified through public laws that institutionalize the fact that killing is in most cases wrong. But how does the distinction between right and wrong come to be? Is it something we are born with or something learned? And how might empathy impact our knowledge of what is right and what is wrong and our subsequent behaviors in light of that knowledge?

Haidt (2012) divides morality into two parts, moral intuition and moral reasoning. Moral intuition comes first. It is automatic and results in almost instantaneous reactions. Moral reasoning follows in a more conscious path that involves justification for our actions and beliefs. This combination reflects both innate and environmental contributors to morality: We are born with an aversion from or an attraction to certain behaviors, and we are taught through our lives which behaviors are considered right and which are considered wrong. This is an interesting proposition. First, it makes moral action both an intuitive reaction and a deliberative thought; second, it reflects the affective and cognitive divide in empathic processing (unconscious affective reaction followed by conscious cognitive deliberation). In fact, the same regions of the brain are activated for empathy and for determining fairness or what we think is right or wrong. The brain regions activated for empathy (particularly in response to the pain of others)—namely, the anterior insula (AI) and the anterior cingulate cortex (ACC)—are the same as those activated when assessing fairness (Singer, 2007). Recent neurological research has found that the ventromedial prefrontal cortex (vmPFC) is also involved in both moral behavior and empathic concern (Decety & Cowell, 2014). Thus, neurologically, empathy and morality seem to be connected or overlapping.

The most comprehensive discussion of the relationship between empathy and morality is found in Hoffman's (2000) work. Hoffman posits that mature adult "affective empathy" (the term he uses to reflect feeling what someone else feels) includes awareness that what you are feeling is in response to someone else's experience and that you are separate from the other (Hoffman, 2011). Hoffman's understanding of empathy, while using somewhat different terminology, for the most part reflects the full scope of empathy as we define it. He discusses morality in relation to empathy from the perspective of consideration for others and he has observed that as a species we would not have survived if people only cared about themselves. Religions, philosophy, and the arts have highlighted the struggle between taking care of oneself and taking care of others. Survival is promoted by balancing these impulses in social interactions, which are informed by empathic insights and guided by morality. Thus, Hoffman considers empathy the "spark of human concern for others" that contributes to caring and a sense of justice, which is a moral judgment. The connection manifests in two possible ways: We react to others who are in distress or suffering, and upon further analysis come to find that the cause of their distress is some kind of unjust treatment or situation, which, in turn, moves us to feel the injustice of their situation; or we already have a sense of what is fair and what is not, and upon meeting or hearing about or imagining a victim of injustice, we empathically feel the unjust treatment (Hoffman, 2000, 2011).

Hoffman (2011) goes on to argue that morality may temper empathy so that while we may feel the distress of another, our moral principles guide our actions vis-à-vis that person. However, sometimes this link involves conflict. Suppose you have a friend who asks you to give a reference for a job where you work, and you know that your friend is not qualified. Your empathic feelings may involve your sharing the friend's deep desire to get a job, but your sense of right and wrong tells you that vouching for your friend when you know there is not a good fit is wrong. You then must decide whether to respond to your empathic feelings and support your friend with a reference, or temper your emotions, choose to do what is "right," and not recommend your friend. Thus, empathy can trigger the process of moral judgments, but the outcome may or may not reflect moral judgement.

On the other hand, moral judgments may affect empathic responses, or the lack thereof. In studies where participants were involved in games with others who were set up to play fairly or unfairly, empathic responses were less for those who played unfairly (Singer, Seymour, O'Doherty, Stephan, Dolan, & Frith, 2006). Our empathic feelings may thus depend on our assessment of whether the person played fairly or not. This is often the case in politics. For example, politicians may claim that they are not against immigrants, but are against those who did not follow the system and play by the rules, those who are considered "illegal" immigrants. This is a reflection of the above phenomenon, that if we perceive people did not play fairly, we have less empathy for them. The situation becomes more complicated if one considers the circumstances to be unjust as opposed to the individuals. If context and history are taken into account, the view may be that people are suffering and want to come to this country to make a better life for themselves, but the law allows only a small number in each year. Helping people in distress would call for increasing the numbers. From that perspective, it is not individuals who are right or wrong, but policies. This helps to explain why we have such political differences on the issue of immigration (and other social issues)—we may share empathic concern for the plight of immigrants, but differ as to whether it is individuals or systems that are right or wrong.

Context can influence moral judgments in very complex ways. In the immigration example above, morality is involved with assessing a political situation. What about when the morals of an individual conflict with the law, at risk of life? For example, why did some individuals break the law during the Holocaust to save people's lives? The story of Anne Frank and her family being hidden and fed by a cohort of Mr. Frank's employees, at great risk to themselves, is the most famous case of personal moral principles taking precedence over law of the land (albeit, this law was imposed on the Dutch by the occupation of German forces). Why do some individuals go against the law or risk their own safety and security to uphold their personal sense of right, wrong, and justice? The answer to the question is very difficult to answer (Turiel, 2015). People seem to weigh personal goals and social goals in distinct ways, within broader social contexts. That may explain why for the most part we behave with a similar moral code, but in some cases we deviate individually. We wonder if part of that deviation is influenced by empathy, drawing us to moral action, or a lack of empathy, leaving us unconnected and unmotivated to take action. Here, social empathy with its attention to understanding context and relevant historical events is important. Social empathy helps us to take a macro perspective-taking view, reducing the distance between ourselves and people of other cultures.

There is evidence that empathy is linked to morality, whether as a trigger for concern or as a dampener of too much concern. However, because views of what is right and wrong can differ, people can say they care about the lives of others (such as immigrants) but come to very different plans for action. It also helps us to see that trying to evoke empathic concern without contextual understanding about a social issue does not always result in greater concern for others, but instead a debate about what is fair or what is right.

Cooperation

Another important area of prosocial behavior is that of cooperation. Cooperation as discussed here means interactions that involve benefits to all who are involved (as opposed to one way, which is more precisely altruism) (Snowdon & Cronin, 2009). As is true for other prosocial behaviors, empathy is important for cooperation. Empathy helps us to "read" other people's emotions and thereby exchange important information. This exchange allows us to live in social groups for the benefit of our own and the species' survival (Carter, Harris, & Porges, 2011). Being understood helps to facilitate communication and working together.

Sharing, a key aspect of cooperation, can be seen in children as young as two years of age, and other prosocial behaviors can be seen as early as in infancy (Dunfield, Kulmeier, O'Connell, & Kelly, 2011). These early abilities suggest that we have a biological predisposition to cooperate. In addition, we are socially taught to cooperate by being rewarded when we do and punished when we do not (Warneken & Tomasello, 2015). Thus, cooperation has biological underpinnings shaped by social learning.

Although empathy may not be an absolute requirement for cooperation, it likely makes the process easier. One reason may be that empathy helps us to overlook unintended behaviors that might otherwise be seen as impeding cooperation (Rumble, Van Lange, & Parks, 2010). For example, picture working on a group project that involves all members following through on their parts in a timely fashion. First, imagine being part of the group and not knowing anyone in the group. When one member does not complete his part of the project on time, you are likely to be annoyed, and not feel great about contributing your part. Now, imagine being part of the group and knowing beforehand that that member's child is sick in the hospital. It is likely that your empathic concern would temper your reaction to his tardiness and you would find a way to work around the lateness of his contribution. In addition to empathy aiding us in understanding the actions and motivations of others, and thereby helping us to survive and be safe, it also helps us develop a deeper understanding of others and their actions and thereby feel more connected and ready to cooperate.

Attachment

Attachment theory posits that humans thrive when they develop a deep and lasting connection to another, particularly as part of child development (Bowlby, 1969). Bowlby's work on attachment theory was based on animal studies that demonstrated that beyond the need to be fed, infants looked for security and safety from a caregiver. In addition, his experience working with children who had been separated from their parents led him to conclude not only that secure attachment serves an evolutionary purpose in that the child's chances at survival are enhanced, but that a strong sense of attachment also helps in future social relations. When one feels secure, one can more readily consider the feelings of others, while when one is insecure, there is very little emotional room to take in the feelings of others (Mikulincer & Shaver, 2015). This makes empathy and attachment related.

The connection between empathy and attachment starts at birth (Decety & Meyer, 2008). When infants find that their behaviors elicit a corresponding response—for example, they cry and are then held or fed—they begin to develop the understanding that there is a connection between them and those around them. When this connection is consistent and includes nurturing (providing security and safety), the child gains a sense of trust that his or her needs will be met in a consistent way. This sense of attachment and security helps the child develop in prosocial ways, which includes the development of empathy. The ability to develop an empathic focus is a result of "having witnessed and benefited from good care provided by one's own attachment figures" (Mikulincer, Shaver, Gillath, & Nitzberg, 2005, p. 818). Such care both provides the base of security and models how to be a good caretaker. Behavioral research on empathy and family relationships supports this assessment of attachment. It provides evidence that family relationships that are close and secure correlate with greater empathic concern (Davis, 1996).

The relationship between empathy and attachment thus goes in two directions. Secure attachment promotes empathic abilities, and an empathic caretaker will be more likely to respond in ways that reinforce the sense of being understood. This early cycle of learning to be empathic may be the foundation for recent studies previously cited that find that imitation strengthens the empathic bond between people. "Being imitated makes people feel more attuned to and connected with others" (van Baaren, Janssen, Chartrand, & Dijksterhuis, 2009, p. 2385). Imitation starts early in life. The ability to share people's experiences likely enhances social connections through better understanding, and knowing that another person reciprocates with empathic insight strengthens the emotional bond between them (de Vignemont & Singer, 2006). The power of attachment to promote empathy, and empathy to promote attachment, while it starts early in life, continues throughout life. This means that even for those whose attachment in childhood was weak or who experienced disruptions to the development of their attachment systems, there is a lifetime to create those neural pathways that are engaged in empathy and attachment (Siegel, 2010).

Emotional Intelligence

In 1994, Daniel Goleman published *Emotional Intelligence*, which made the case for the importance of being attuned to our feelings as well as the feelings of others. Viewing this skill as a form of intelligence, he contended that when we develop it, we have the tools to promote individual and social well-being. He outlined five domains of emotional intelligence (EI): knowing one's own emotions, managing one's emotions, motivating oneself, recognizing emotions in others, and handling relationships. Although our definition of the full scope of empathy covers several of these areas, he considered recognizing emotions in others as the domain of empathy. In fact, he devoted an entire chapter to empathy. Critics argue that because emotional intelligence is a collection of numerous social and emotional skills, it is difficult to identify an agreed-upon definition or description, and consequently measurement instruments vary greatly making it difficult to assess emotional intelligence (Cherniss, 2010; Conte, 2005). In spite of the broad scope of EI, we applaud the attention and importance that emotional intelligence has brought to empathy. However, it is important not to let empathy dissolve into emotional intelligence, which can be rather vague. Empathy is a neurologically identifiable ability, which means we can track it, measure it, and teach it.

TOO MUCH EMPATHY?

With so many positive aspects of empathy, is there a downside? New research raises such an interesting question (Righetti, Hofmann, Gere, Visserman & Van Lange, 2016). Are highly empathic people more likely to have negative reactions when their interest diverges from the preference of their romantic partners? Or in simple terms, does a higher level of empathic concern mean that when differing with someone very close to them, people feel greater disappointment and stress? And if so, what impact might that have on the relationship? Researchers followed over one hundred couples for eight days, having them report in via smartphone several times a day on questions about instances of divergence with their partner, their mood, and relationship satisfaction. Each person had already taken a baseline test in empathic concern. The study findings suggest that those with higher levels of empathy were more negatively affected by having differences with their partner and felt the discomfort more deeply. Does this put the relationship at risk, or does it simply mean that more empathic individuals experience others' emotions more deeply, something we already know to be true? On a positive note, at one year follow-up, relationship satisfaction did not change in relation to the divergence of interests. Thus, the impact in the moment may be more stressful, but over time it may not have a negative impact on relationship satisfaction.

This is only one study, but it raises an important question. Does having a higher level of empathy make one more susceptible to the experience of deeper emotions that at times can be stressful and leave one in a negative mood? We know that in empathically responding to another's pain or sadness, self-other awareness and emotional regulation are crucial. To what extent can we count on those abilities to temper strong emotional reactions? In the study, only the construct of empathic concern was measured. This means that the definition of empathy used in the research did not necessarily reflect the full scope of empathy as we define it. Without knowing how well individuals can maintain self-other awareness and regulate emotions to protect themselves from the intensity of feeling another's emotions, we cannot answer that question. But given that the participants did not register a change in relationship satisfaction over time, we might conclude that while those with greater empathic concern may feel divergence stress more deeply, they can also handle it over time. This research emphasizes why it is helpful to understand empathy as a combination of components, each contributing important aspects to the full scope of empathy.

WHAT ABOUT COMPASSION?

Up until this point, we have not specifically addressed the concept of compassion and its relationship to empathy and prosocial behavior. Recall from chapter 1 that compassion is typically concern for another person who is in distress and that while often used as a synonym for empathy, it is not the same. "In contrast to empathy, compassion does not mean sharing the suffering of the other: rather, it is characterized by feelings of warmth, concern and care for the other, as well as a strong motivation to improve the other's wellbeing" (Singer & Klimecki, 2014, p. R875). It is the difference between "feeling as another" (empathy) and "feeling for another" (compassion). "Compassion arises in response to appraisals of suffering" (Goetz, Keltner, & Simon-Thomas, 2010, p. 363). This definition means that we can have compassion through cerebral processing without emotional engagement.

We take the position that empathy might trigger compassion, which can lead to action, but the appraisal process behind compassion is not instigated by sharing affective stimuli. If the full scope of empathy, which includes perspective-taking, is engaged, it may overlap with compassion. Once we put ourselves in the place of the other, we may be moved to take action to help minimize the other's distress. Because compassion is concerned only with the suffering of others and can operate cognitively without sharing the other's experience, we think it is prone to hierarchical responses, that is, providing care or support in a patronizing way placing the giver in a controlling position over the receiver. Such a hierarchical relationship may not be truly helpful and instead can breed resentment on both sides—for the giver a feeling of "look what I have done for you and you do not appreciate it" or for the receiver "I feel looked down on as a failure because I am in need." When we do not put ourselves in the place of others, we run the risk of misinterpreting the other and considering what would alleviate our own suffering, not what works for the other. There is a long history of more dominant cultures having compassion for those who are suffering and expressing that compassion in paternalistic and controlling ways. For example, early on, orphanages for impoverished children that stressed hygiene and health with little emotional or physical engagement with the children were thought to show compassion by those who championed the care, though they lacked empathic insight. Engagement of the full scope of interpersonal and social empathy guards against such mistaken approaches.

WHAT DO WE KNOW ABOUT A LACK OF EMPATHY?

A discussion on why empathy is important would not be complete without considering what it means when people lack empathy. A lack of empathy is not just a lack of prosocial behaviors; it can also mean a preponderance of antisocial behaviors. Behaviors such as bullying (Gini, Albiero, Benelli, & Altoe, 2008), spousal battering (Covell, Huss, & Langhinrichsen-Rohling, 2007), and sexual offending (Elsegood & Duff, 2010) have all been linked to an absence of empathy or diminished empathy. Research on the personal and social cost of a lack of empathy is extensive—there are books dedicated to the analysis of antisocial behaviors that reflect a lack of empathy (for example, Baron-Cohen, 2011). In this section we will review some of the research concerning a lack of empathy that reinforces why empathy is so important. In the next chapter we explore in more detail what it means for human relations and society when people and groups are deficient in their sense of empathy.

A lack of empathy is most linked to psychopathy. Although definitions of *psychopathy* vary, making it challenging to determine how empathy is impacted by those who are categorized as psychopathic, there is agreement that psychopathy includes a deficit in empathy. Recent conceptualizations regard psychopathy as a coming together of three distinct traits: boldness, which involves dominance and fearlessness; meanness, or callousness and self-interestedness, with no regard for consequences or for others; and disinhibition, which is a lack of emotion regulation (Almeida et al., 2015). Immediately, without delving further into the research, we can see that these three characteristics present barriers to empathy. First, dominance and self-interest preclude putting yourself in another's situation. Second, a lack of emotion regulation precludes any processing of the emotions that arise with affective response, mentalizing, self-other awareness, and perspective-taking. Indeed, several neuroimaging studies have found that the brain patterns related to empathy do not operate as expected for those with psychopathic traits. Decety, Chen, Harenski, and Kiehl (2013) found that in people categorized as psychopaths, there is an interesting split: while their brains process imagining of their own affects in a way that is consistent with empathic individuals, they differ during third-person perspective-taking. When asked to process the feelings or experiences of others, those who were identified as psychopaths did not recruit the orbitofrontal cortex (OFC) region of the brain, nor couple it with the amygdala, as would be the case in situations involving moral judgments and empathy. These findings corroborate earlier research that also found dysfunction in the amygdala and OFC of youths with psychopathic traits (Marsh et al., 2011). Data suggest that with psychopathy, the amygdala seems to be less responsive to stimuli, thereby creating a deficit in learning about good and bad actions; likewise, there is also less response in the OFC, which means moral decision-making is disrupted or impaired (Blair 2007; Blair 2010; Blair & White, 2013). It is not necessarily that psychopathology blocks all assessment of others. Mentalizing means drawing inferences about other people's thinking and interpreting their affective states, but it does not involve emotional engagement in the way that empathy does. This may be why psychopaths can understand the mental workings of others, which makes them good at manipulating those others, but they are deficient in the emotional aspects of empathy (Singer & Decety, 2011).

The link between psychopathy and a deficiency in empathy contributes to our understanding of why some antisocial people can behave in ways that disregard the feelings and needs of others, and why they are viewed as lacking a moral conscience. Although research has documented this neurological processing difference, understanding how it comes to be or how to train people with psychopathic traits to become empathic is the next frontier. Such treatment will likely require a combination of interventions, both cognitive and biological. Promising findings suggest that combining the two can have an impact on changing actual brain patterns in people with psychological disorders (Crocker, Heller, Warren, O'Hare, Infantolino, & Miller, 2013), given the neuroplasticity of our brains. As the next section highlights, human beings have evolved to become more connected to others beyond their kin groups and gained greater emotional awareness in the process as well. This historic shift demonstrates that brain patterns can change over time. The challenge today is to better understand and harness that evolutionary change pattern to work for individuals whose brain functions lack the neural connections to be empathic.

CIVILIZATION AND EMPATHY

One of the responses we may feel when we hear news of violence and egregious acts of maltreatment is that we need empathy on a global scale. In some ways this is not a new message. Admonitions for self-other awareness and perspective-taking in the treatment of others date back thousands of years. Major religions teach consideration of others: Both the Old and the New Testaments say, "Love your neighbor as yourself" (Leviticus 19:18, Mark 12:31, Luke 10:27); Confucius, the great Chinese philosopher, wrote "Do not do to others what you would not like them to do to you." (Waley, 1989, p. 68). Likewise, the Jewish philosopher Hillel observed, "What is hateful to you do not do unto thy fellow," (Rodkinson, 1903, p. 50) while Hindu sacred literature states, "Let no man do to another that which would be repugnant to himself" (Mahabharta, n.d.). This is not an exhaustive list of historical texts asking us to imagine ourselves in the place of another and caring about how we treat the other, but it does demonstrate the embeddedness of such perspectives across different cultures.

Although the message may not be new, the medium through which we can build global empathy is new. Never before in history have we been so connected across geographical distances as we are today, thanks to advances in technology. We can talk on the phone or instant message with anyone just about anywhere with the help of orbiting satellites. We can see others over computers, cell phones, tablets, and other modes of video transmission—and do so in real time. But can all these new ways of opening and connecting the world promote global empathy?

Jeremy Rifkin, the author of *The Empathic Civilization* (2009), sees an evolution in empathic abilities that has taken place as a part of, and as a consequence of, the history of civilization. He wrote the book to document and encourage recognition of our shared world so that we can tap into our empathic consciousness, and by building on it, generate global empathy. He writes that we have progressed toward a greater "empathic consciousness" in terms of the way we support parenting and attachment to our children, by having more exposure to different people, groups, and cultures, and as a result of increased global economic connections. He also sees a connection between empathy and the growth in democracy:

> The ability to recognize oneself in the other and the other in oneself is a deeply democratizing experience. Empathy is the soul of democracy. It is the acknowledgment that each life is unique, unalienable, and deserving of equal consideration in the public square. The evolution of empathy and the evolution of democracy have gone hand in hand throughout history. The more empathic the culture, the more democratic its values and government institutions. The less empathic the culture, the more totalitarian its values and governing institutions. (p. 161)

Rifkin's worry is that while our empathic civilization has been growing, so too have the degradation of our climate and the proliferation of weapons of mass destruction. Special care is needed to increase attention to our interconnectedness and the need for global empathy. For us, this is where social empathy built on a foundation of interpersonal empathy can provide a blueprint for addressing Rifkin's concerns.

The Decline in Violence and Unempathic Behaviors

Sometimes when we see the daily news, it feels like there is a decline in empathy—terrorist attacks, stalkers killing victims, children dying at the hands of their caretakers—it can and does overwhelm us. When weighing the extent of empathy in our world, it helps to take a broader view of history and see where we are today versus where we were hundreds, even thousands of years ago. Psychologist and linguist Steven Pinker (2011) has chronicled the history of violence over the past several thousand years, and with the use of data and painstaking analysis, his deeply researched conclusion is that violence has declined over history and continues to decline. He regards the evolution of humanity from competition between tribes and clans to the cooperation for shared economic gain under the protection and support of organized communities, what he cites as the growth of city-states as contributing to the decline in violence. Fighting over resources is a zero-sum exchange in that the one who wins gains, but the one who loses has nothing. This perpetuates a cycle of plunder, which usually requires force. However, trading resources and technologies are positive-sum exchanges; both groups gain and do so without needing force. If one group consists of farmers who have extra grain at the end of the harvest, and another group consists of shepherds who have extra sheep after the mating season, exchanging what each group has in surplus adds to and enhances each group's total resources. If one group plunders and burns the other's fields or grazing land, they still have their own surplus, but lose the opportunity for exchange because they destroyed the other's surplus. Economic exchanges have the added benefit of enhancing cultural exchanges, and those who can communicate best with others who are different, gain the most. Hence insight into the thinking and needs of others has been reinforced by the development of commerce. And with the development of commerce has been the development of structures and systems such as governments and rules regarding trade.

Larger government bodies are needed to make possible the infrastructure to support economic exchange, as well as to monitor and regulate such exchanges. The result is a more urbane civilization that promotes trade, technology, science, humanism, and protection of individual rights. All of these advances have led to a decline in violence. Contributing to that reduction in violence has been increased empathy. Both Pinker and Rifkin cite the economic advancement of human history as paving the way for technological advancements, with the most significant advance being the written word. Both regard literacy as the reason for growth in human empathy. Rifkin regards print communication as the pathway to connect people in new ways across broader distances. Pinker cites the evolution of the printing press and making literature accessible as being a means for more and more people coming to be able to engage in perspective-taking. He documents that the growth in literacy accompanied, and likely contributed to a decline in violence, reasoning that:

> Stepping into someone else's vantage point reminds you that the other fellow [sic] has a first-person, present-tense, ongoing stream of consciousness that

is very much like your own but not the same as your own. It's not a big leap to suppose that the habit of reading other people's words could put one in the habit of entering other people's minds, including their pleasures and pains. Slipping even for a moment into the perspective of someone who is turning black in a pillory [reflecting a form of popular torture through history] or desperately pushing burning faggots away from her body [as was done to burn women considered to be witches] or convulsing under the two hundredth stroke of the lash [as was done to punish slaves] may give a person second thoughts as to whether these cruelties should ever be visited upon anyone. Adopting other people's vantage points can alter one's convictions. (p. 175)

And indeed, Pinker's book is an in-depth accounting of how far from these practices much of the world has come. He notes that this evolution has been uneven, and at times has taken steps back: the Holocaust and genocide in Rwanda are two modern examples of the latter. He warns that in places where people live in collective misfortune and chaos, where young men are unemployed and disconnected from opportunities to participate in nurturing and raising children, and where leaders emerge to promote an ideology that promises a perfect world, the attraction to that ideology can be strong. It also means that anyone standing in the way of that ideology must be stopped or eliminated, at any cost. Although Pinker's book came out before the rise of the Islamic State (ISIS or ISIL), his analysis of what gives rise to societies ruled by violence describes exactly the circumstances surrounding the rise of ISIS. He argues that one of the antidotes to violence is empathy. When people can expand their understanding of others through literacy, experience, travel, and socializing, they can come to the place of wanting to treat others as they would want others to treat them. The challenge is that only safety and security can ensure that the ingredients for empathy are open to all, and that can be difficult in closed or isolated communities that are in chaos politically, socially, and economically.

Prosocial Behavior and Culture

As we see from Pinker's study of the decline in violence throughout history and Rifkin's chronicle of the evolution of a greater empathic consciousness, progress towards building empathy over time and across the world is possible.

Prosocial behavior is "embedded in the fabric of cultures" (Feygina & Henry, 2015, p. 201). As members of a social group or culture, we are exposed to beliefs and practices that we internalize as we grow up. Likewise, context is important for the development of our own empathic abilities and ability to understand the circumstances of others. When the context in which we live is stable and safe, interpersonal interactions and exchanges can progress and prosper. Then we can engage in cross-cultural exchanges that promote social empathy.

Lamm and Majdandžić (2015) warn that the increase in public attention to empathy may be simplifying a complex process and presenting a solution to global problems that is too simplistic. Increasing empathic abilities alone may not bring about increased social empathic consciousness. They point out that because of our proclivity to be more empathic toward those whom we know, we would benefit from expanding our social groups and those whom we consider to be like us. We agree that is one way to build an empathic civilization, and developing wider personal experiences of diversity is critical and advantageous. But with the breadth of world communities, it may not be realistic in practice.

The world is large and complex, and no matter how many YouTube videos we might view or online groups we might join, there are still wide cultural differences that cannot be understood or bridged without intense interpersonal experience. When we cannot expand our personal experiences, we need to engage our cognitive processing to include understanding of context and history. We need to mentally participate in cultural perspective-taking for groups who are different from us. This may require the help of specialists who can provide us with information on context, history, and perspectives of those who are different. It can be furthered by hearing the first-hand stories of those whose lived experiences are different. To mentally expand our social groups where we cannot physically do so—that could extend our empathic abilities and go far toward connecting people around the globe.

4

Why Is Empathy So Difficult to Achieve?

THE BIOLOGICAL DRIVE BEHIND KIN SELECTION AND ALTRUISM, coupled with our unconscious affective response and activation of the mirror neuron system, suggest that there is an innate drive toward empathy for all human beings. We have already discussed how empathy helps survival, promotes cooperation, and has played a part in the expansion of civilizations. Given such a fundamental role in human existence, why have there been so many lapses in empathy throughout human history? We discussed the impact of some mental health issues such as psychopathy and the differences in brain processing, both of which partly help to explain why some individuals lack empathy. But why is history full of examples of widespread, organized actions that demonstrate lack of empathy? How do we accept that the ability to empathize is innate, considering genocide, holocaust, torture, ethnic cleansings, atomic bombings, human trafficking, and so many other examples of dehumanization and violence? This may be the most important question about empathy. If we can understand why and how human beings behave in such a way as to show no empathy, then we will have better insight about how to overcome those lapses and teach and enhance people's empathic abilities and actions.

BARRIERS TO EMPATHY

Numerous characteristics of human beings seem to conflict with being empathic. A large part of empathy requires cognitive processing, which is conscious and implies a choice of whether to engage or not. Of course, that "choice" might be blocked by biologically dysfunctional brain processing, or social learning to ignore certain feelings or thoughts, or so much stress from environmental factors that people cannot see beyond their own situations. A lack of empathy might even be a result of brain processing being hijacked from other unconscious parts of our brain, as in cases where fear paralyzes us in a way that impedes cognitive processing. In this chapter we review the numerous individual and group obstacles that make engaging empathically a challenge for human beings.

Otherness, the Downside to Tribal Identity

Ironically, the strongest push for empathy also works against it. That is, while empathy is related to the connection we feel toward those we know and those who are similar to us, weak empathy or an absence of empathy is related to the lack of connection with others whom we do not know and who are different from us. This distinction is often referred to in research as the phenomenon of *ingroup* and *outgroup* identity. Before the use of neuroimaging, numerous studies found a prevalence of ingroup bias, or favoritism, even when the group identities were set up randomly and carried meaningless labels, such as membership in the green group as opposed to the blue group (Brewer, 1979).

The most salient point to take away from this early body of research is that the tendency for ingroup favoritism was stronger than negative feelings or hostility toward outgroup members. These tendencies suggested that being a part of a group was the impetus for preferential treatment of other group members, rather than as a result of a dislike of outsiders from an outgroup. In action it may be that empathy motivates our ingroup helping while outgroup helping tends to reflect more of a social exchange, that is engaging in relations or transactions that are for the benefit of both groups (Stürmer & Snyder, 2010). Social exchange does not deny empathic feelings, but may reflect cognitively directed efforts such as weighing the pros and cons of helping someone who is different and from another group.

Since the earlier observational and self-report studies were conducted, additional research using measures of brain activity through functional magnetic resonance imaging (fMRI) has shown that we tend to activate the same brain regions and have higher levels of empathic understanding for those who are similar to us (Eres & Molenberghs, 2013). In some studies, the difference between ingroup and outgroup empathy was not necessarily in the level of empathy, but in how the observer got there. In a study of brain mechanism responses to social suffering (friends or strangers being left out of a cyberball game), researchers found that observers experienced brain activations of regions associated with first-hand pain when seeing the exclusion of their friends (Meyer et al., 2013). However, when observing the social exclusion of strangers, the brain mechanisms that were activated were for mentalizing or second-hand pain. Thus, the empathy was there, but the brain activation patterns differed, suggesting that we may have a more affective and unconscious empathic link to those whom we know as opposed to a more conscious social learned empathic link for those whom we do not know. Even the simple task of recognizing emotional expressions (such as happiness, sadness, fear) was more accurate among ingroup members even when the affiliation of the group was random and not based on any previous social group characteristic (Young & Hugenberg, 2010). Empathy for others may need the cognitive elements of self-other awareness, perspective-taking, and possibly emotion regulation more than empathy for those whom we know well or who are part of our ingroup.

The power of otherness to block empathy is particularly strong when we have a social aversion instilled in us, such as prejudice based on race or ethnicity or stigmas related to social outcasts. These barriers suggest there is a strong learned component that may reinforce the biological kin selection bias and diminish or block empathy for outgroup members. If empathy is likely to be both biological and socially learned, so might diminished empathy be. In the next section we review a number of relevant studies and the salient points about human reactions to "otherness" (those who are different) and ingroup versus outgroup empathy, as well as the social learning aspects of empathy and otherness.

GROUP IDENTITY

Research has identified human preferences for empathy toward fellow group members. This makes a lot of sense from an evolutionary perspective: Understanding and responding to the needs of others helps in the survival of social groups (de Waal, 2009). Tribes relied on their members for protection, collection of food, and rearing of young. Without that mutual support, survival is much more difficult, if not impossible. The tendency for greater empathy within social groups has been documented through numerous studies (examples include Brown, Bradley, & Lang, 2006; Gutsell & Inzlicht, 2012; Hein, Silani, Preuschoff, Batson, & Singer, 2010; Mathur, Harada, Lipke, & Chiao, 2010; O'Brien & Ellsworth, 2012). People tend to have greater levels of empathic concern for others who are similar to them and with whom they have more familiarity. This too makes evolutionary sense. Growing up, an individual is typically surrounded by kin and those who share the same group identity. These are the people who are most likely going to help one survive and prosper. If there is competition between groups for resources needed for survival, then the biological proclivity will be reinforced by the social learning parts of empathy—we feel for and help those related to our survival, but do not have those same feelings for those who may endanger our survival. Thus, the split in empathy for those we know versus those whom we do not know may be more cognitive than affective, but learned at such a young age that it may feel innate to us.

The strength of these connections is not surprising given the numerous examples throughout history of group solidarity based on shared attributes, as well as group animosity based on group differences. History is full of examples of "us" versus "them," or "othering," that served as the impetus behind building solidarity and union, as well as fueling wars and ethnic disputes. When it comes to the strength of group identity, this may be a trait that has been passed on genetically as well as socially. That is, it is likely that communities or tribal groups with higher levels of empathy for their own members prospered and passed that attribute on. For example, collectivist societies, those that encourage and favor social harmony and consider people very connected to each other, which is a manifestation of understanding the needs of others, have lower prevalence of anxiety and depressive disorders (Chiao & Blizinsky, 2010). The researchers suggest that this may be due in part to support for empathic understanding as a shared value. The question then arises, if empathic societies grew and passed this trait on within their own group, how does empathy pass beyond those with whom we are already familiar?

For survival purposes, although the tendency of "othering" may seem set, in fact it may well be fluid. People make shifts in group identity that can override long-standing commonalities. For example, in research where temporary group identifications were arbitrarily manufactured, dominant group identity such as race became secondary (Van Bavel & Cunningham, 2009). Each of us has multiple identities (we are male or female, member of dominant or non-dominant race, born to one of many difference religions, etc.) and have likely experienced times in our lives when being one identity felt more important or pronounced than another, yet we were still the same person as a whole. The ability to develop a new group identity that overrides a current identity suggests a strong cognitive element behind ingroup versus outgroup empathy.

Relating more empathically to members of a group to which you belong can develop based on an immediate sense of group identity, which can even override long-standing group identities. This notion has been supported by neurological imaging. Lamm, Meltzoff, and Decety (2009) compared observers' neural reactions to watching allegedly neurological patients with a disorder that caused them pain when they were touched by soft objects such as a cotton swab and no pain when they were pricked by sharp objects such as a needle. For the observers, seeing an action that would be painful to them but was not to the patients, and vice versa, involved a cognitive reversal of interpretation. The goal of the research was to see what happens with empathy if you are dissimilar to others in a way that does not reflect your own previously learned differences. By making up the condition, pain from a cotton swab and no pain from a needle, there would be no prior social learning relevant to the conditions used in the study, although the observers were required to revise what they already knew about the objects. The results of the fMRIs showed that it is more challenging to share the physical affect when told that the action is not painful to the participant, but is identified as painful by the observer—that is, watching the needle injection into a person who supposedly does not experience pain from the needle injection took cognitive regulation and control to suppress the affective experience of pain. We might surmise from this that if we are cognitively prepped to view others in a certain way, we can counter our affective responses to adjust to the cognitive "story" we have been told. In some ways, this may be the process that doctors and other medical professionals need to learn in order to not be affectively and emotionally overrun by the conditions of ailing patients (Decety, Yang, & Cheng, 2010). In such cases, being able to cognitively override affective responses is a good thing. However, doing so because we are taught to dislike another group, on the basis of race, religion, or other factors is not socially helpful.

Another reason empathy gets blocked might be our tendency to project our own mental states onto others. Silani, Lamm, Ruff, and Singer (2013) examined this phenomenon, which they refer to as *emotional egocentricity bias* (EEB). They found that affective resonance, or the understanding of the feelings of others by experiencing the affective state through mirroring, can be biased by our interpretation of what that state means to us. Therefore, we still need to use other neural pathways to clarify whether what we are feeling is indeed what the observed other is feeling. Through fMRIs they identified the additional brain area that was involved when people needed to disengage from their own experience when it seemed to conflict with what they cognitively processed as actually being experienced by the other. They suggest that we likely need to draw on self-other awareness to overcome our EEB and to inhibit potential mistaken assessment of the other person's experience. Thus, what research tells us is that while empathy is important to people and is shared within groups, it is also malleable. This has important implications for teaching empathy and promoting connections between people from different social groups. Before we look at the malleability of group identity and self-other awareness, we should note that there are several attitudes and behaviors that are particularly strong in diminishing empathy. The power of prejudice and stigma to block the ability to feel for and with another is one. And given the longstanding existence of these barriers to empathy, we also need to examine how malleable ingrained beliefs are in regard to promoting empathy.

RACE, INGROUP IDENTITY, AND DIMINISHED EMPATHY

Race is an observable difference between groups, and as such has played a significant role in history in dividing people by groups. It is also likely that race plays a role in how we empathically perceive others. Using fMRI, Xu, Zuo, Wang, and Han (2009) compared the brain reactions of a group of Chinese students to those of a group of Caucasian students when viewing pictures of members of both groups receiving a painful injection. They found increased activity in the neural circuits expressing first-hand pain experience when observing the painful pictures of same-race faces for both groups, and lesser degrees of activation when viewing outgroup members. Also using fMRI scans, Mathur, Harada, Lipke, and Chiao (2010) found that African American and Caucasian American participants responded with similar affective neural activity when observing others in pain, but added additional cognitive neural processes when the pain was observed in members of their own social group. In another experiment, researchers used transcranial magnetic simulation (TMS) to track changes in brain activity of white and black participants (Avenanti, Sirigu, & Aglioti, 2010). When participants viewed videos of white, black, and purple hands being pricked with needles or touched by cotton swabs, and affective responses for pain and touch were compared, several interesting findings emerged. The basic reactivity of human beings is to be empathic, that is, to affectively share the pain of others, even those without any existence in reality, as in the purple hands. However, it is strongest with regard to those who are similar to us (ingroup members), weaker with regard to the neutral purple hands, and weakest with regard to others who are of a different race. Also, the processing of the image of a hand from an outgroup member took longer, thereby demonstrating more immediate connections with same-race members. Separately, the researchers also tested participants on their level of racial bias, and found that empathic affective sharing was weakest or nonexistent for those who tested high on racial bias. Their results suggest that affective empathy is present even with members of other groups, but where there is cultural conditioning, that is, the learning of bias such as racism and categorization of outgroup status, such attitudes may impede resonance with others who are different. In other words, it appears that we learn to cognitively turn off or ignore any automatic shared experience with an "other" group if our social learning includes bias and prejudice toward that group. These findings are corroborated by the work of Gutsell and Inzlicht (2010, 2012) who found the neural networks involved in action simulation and understanding intention are less responsive to outgroup members, and especially so for prejudiced people. They suggest that although there may naturally be a propensity to neurologically resonate more with ingroup members, prejudice might activate a cognitive bias to not be attentive to disliked groups and not find them relevant enough to process what they are feeling. If the lack of attention is based in cognitive processing, then enhancing perspective-taking might compensate for or shift inattention due to prejudice.

After reviewing studies of race and social brain functioning, Chiao and Mathur (2010) agree with the malleability of the neural processes for racial bias in empathy. They concluded that "racial bias in empathic neural responses is not inevitable, but instead results from culturally acquired prejudice. This in turn demonstrates flexibility in empathic neural circuitry and highlights a pivotal role for culture in changing how and when humans share and respond to the suffering of same and other races" (pp. R479—R480).

We conclude from these studies that at least in regard to racial bias, there are cognitive ways to address impeded empathy. It may not be easy to introduce these interventions to people who hold strong beliefs about other races, but considering the historical damage from racism to societies and individuals, this is encouraging. What about other biases? Is the brain malleable to effect empathy for others who are different based on stigmatized characteristics?

SOCIAL STIGMA AND OUTGROUP STATUS

Empathy for others is also influenced by how we perceive them in terms of groupings that are socially constructed. People are placed in outgroups based on temporary conditions, such as being homeless, or move into outgroups due to a change in their lives, such as becoming HIV positive. Outgroups often are stigmatized, which may be a combination of evolutionary aversion (for example, wanting to stay away from disease) and socially constructed thinking based in otherness (Pryor, Reeder, Monroe, & Patel, 2010). Similar beliefs often lead to group identity, such as being a member of a political party or advocacy group—an ingroup—which then results in facing opposing groups—outgroups—also formed on the basis of political beliefs and positions. Consequently, some of our group identities are chosen, like political party affiliation, some are innate, such as race or ethnicity, and some are external to the person, such as being homeless. When it comes to outside groups, how we view them shapes how much empathy we have for them.

In general, we seem to have less empathy when misfortune happens to others whom we regard negatively. For example, participants in a study were presented with two groups, one that they expressed envy toward, such as rich business people, and one they felt pity for, such as elderly people or people with disabilities, with the same misfortune occurring to both groups. The participants' levels of self-reported empathy were lower for the envied group (Cikara & Fiske, 2011). Thus, it may be that our ingroup/outgroup differences in empathy are more nuanced and are moderated by other factors. For example, our stigmatizing of certain groups may be a function of our perception of how they got to be a member of such group.

In a brain imaging study designed to explore the shared neural experience of healthy individuals and those who were identified as having AIDS, researchers found that it mattered what the circumstances of AIDS transmission were (Decety, Echols, & Correll, 2009). When viewing videos depicting three different groups of people experiencing pain from a middle-ear disorder, one group had the disorder but were otherwise healthy, a second group had the disorder and also had AIDS that had been contracted via an infected blood transfusion, and the third group had the disorder and had AIDS that had been contracted through sharing infected needles while using illegal intravenous drugs. Participants' brain activity, as measured through fMRI scans, showed the greatest sensitivity to pain for the people with AIDS transmitted through infected blood transfusions. Using additional measures, the researchers compared these results with participants' perceived levels of blame or responsibility for actions or situations and found that the more that blame was attached to individuals, the less pain and empathy for them observers reported experiencing.

Again using pain as the evocative emotion, participants in another study were asked to imagine the feelings of four different groups experiencing a painful experience: themselves, a most loved person familiar to them, a most hated person familiar to them, and a stranger (Bucchioni, Lelard, Ahmaidi, Godefroy, Krystkowiak, & Mouras, 2015). Ratings on pain were highest for the most loved person, followed by the self, then the stranger, and then the most hated person. Interestingly, the reaction time to assess the pain was shortest for the stranger, then the self, followed by the most loved person, with the longest reaction time recorded for the most hated person. The researchers hypothesized that the longer reaction time may have been a consequence of inhibiting any congruent feelings with the person most hated. The possibility for such cognitive processing is in keeping with the cognitive work that seems to go into suppressing racial bias as discussed in the previous section.

What might we learn about empathy from these studies? Using cognitive processing such as an observer considering how much an individual might be responsible for his or her situation or an observer taking into account his or her relationship to the observed, may affect our levels of empathy. Such might have been the case with the views of people with AIDS— the circumstances of their infection (if they themselves were seen as being to blame for getting infected) gives us a cognitive reason to distance ourselves from them. In the other study, the delay in time for reacting to the pain of those who were hated might reflect that cognitive processing, too. Distancing ourselves based on our assumption of responsibility might be true for our perceptions of homeless persons: Differentiating between someone who is homelessness because his employer went out of business and he lost his job and someone who is homeless because he is an alcoholic and lost his job, we might feel more empathy for the first person because he was a victim of circumstances outside his control compared to the perceived choices made by the second person.

The cognitive processing of our emotions might sway our empathy. A study looking at people's inferences of others' emotions following Hurricane Katrina provides evidence that interpretations of emotions for ingroup members differs from those of outgroup members (Cuddy, Rock, & Norton, 2007). Starting with the difference between primary emotions, which are shared by humans and animals (examples include pain, fear, pleasure) and secondary emotions, which are uniquely felt by humans (such as mourning, admiration, disappointment), the authors found that participants viewed outgroup victims of the storm as experiencing fewer secondary emotions than ingroup victims, although they saw both groups as similar in terms of primary emotions such as fear and sadness. We suspect that the primary emotions triggered affective responses, while the secondary emotions involved cognitive processing. Using cognitive processing to assess whether someone is experiencing secondary emotions may include making the assumption that out group members are different and therefore do not share those secondary emotions.

In addition, the researchers found that the lower levels of inferring secondary emotions were related to reduced intentions to help with Hurricane Katrina relief efforts. Although the research considered only intentions and not whether they actually influenced actions, it does raise some interesting question. Do we tend to see outgroup members as less human than we are, which permits us to feel less empathy, or do we feel less empathy because of being different from them and therefore assuming that they cannot have complex emotions like those of our own group? Either way, the lesson from this research is that when we see other groups as less human than ourselves, we feel more distance and are less likely to be helpful or empathic.

These research findings suggest that we need to find ways to enhance the cognitive processing that helps us to see the humanity of others, rather than view their identity in terms of a condition or social construction (AIDS patient, homeless person, and so on). This line of thinking may be behind fundraising campaigns that highlight individual's personal stories (such as children) rather than describe the conditions of entire groups. If we can connect to the member of another group as an individual human being as opposed to a nondescript member of a group that differs from us, we might be able to enhance empathy between members of different groups.

POSITIONS OF POWER AND EMPATHY

An additional category of otherness we often encounter is difference based on power. Power in our society is reflected in the extent of one's control over situations and others, social and economic position, and class background, as well as the depth of one's belief in the appropriateness of social dominance, which describes the phenomenon of one group having control over others. Research has shown that a person's level of power is connected with different expressions of and capacities for empathy, such that while power can be accompanied by lower empathy, those in power can be more empathic, but only if they feel responsible for those who have less power or they already value being empathic. All three perspectives show that power and empathy are linked.

We know that empathy is key to promoting helping behaviors. Ironically, helping situations may increase the differentiation of power. Those in need of help are typically in lower strata, hence the reason they need help. Those in positions to help typically have more resources or control over resources than those in need. Thus, the helping relationship by its nature includes a power differential (Nadler, 2010). Because so many situations that involve help rely on empathic concern, the extent to which those in power have lower levels of empathy means that the connection between those in need and those with the resources to help is fragile. For example, if those in political power are making decisions for those who are poor, and doing so without benefit of empathic insight, the resulting policies and programs are likely to be a bad fit, not what is actually needed (see Segal, 2006 for a discussion of this mismatch as evidenced by welfare policies).

It may not seem surprising that those in power are more self-focused and not all that concerned about those who lack such power. Research measuring brain activity to determine resonance with others did find that participants primed for high power (recalling a memory when they felt power over someone else immediately before participating in the experiment) had lower levels of motor resonance or mirroring of others compared to low-power participants (Hogeveen, Inzlicht, & Obhi, 2014). If individuals experience less mirroring, then the ability to empathize is reduced, and indeed the researchers concluded that "the default effect of high power appears to be reduced interpersonal sensitivity" (p. 5). Those with power perform worse in another key component of empathy, perspective-taking. Over four different experiments, participants who were primed with high power showed less comprehension of how other people see, think, and feel (Galinsky, Magee, Inesi, & Gruenfeld, 2006). The high-power participants were less likely to take another's perspective, and in fact, power was an impediment to perspective-taking. Those with power were less focused on others and what their experiences might mean, and were more self-focused. It is possible that this self-focus helps those in power to stay attentive to tasks and stay in control, but it also makes empathic insight into others less likely. While considering sources of influence, Van Kleef, Oveis, Homan, van der Löwe, and Keltner (2015) asked powerful people who influenced them more, themselves or others. They found that the powerful prefer to attend to their own experiences rather than those of other people. This tendency re-inforces the earlier findings that those with power are less likely to engage in perspective-taking. Taken together, these research findings suggest that people with power are less likely to engage in empathy. However, research suggests that not all people in power are less likely to engage in perspective-taking. Using a physiological indicator of prosocial orientation (heart and respiration rate, as used in numerous other studies linking the rate to having a prosocial orientation) the researchers found that if one already has a proso-cial orientation, then higher levels of empathic accuracy are found among those with power (Côté et al., 2011). The authors conclude that power may enhance existing tendencies. If a person is already prosocially motivated, then having power helps the person to act accordingly and results in higher levels of empathic accuracy, that is, in sensing and understanding the emo-tions of others.

Another kind of power rests in social class. Those who are members of higher socioeconomic groups have more resources, education, and higher employment rates, all of which mean that they have more control and hence power. In comparisons of people who differ by economic background, those who come from low-income backgrounds display higher levels of empathic accuracy (being able to correctly judge the emotions of another person) than those who come from high-income backgrounds (Kraus, Côté, & Keltner, 2010). It seems that with a lack of resources and control, those who identify as lower-class are more used to focusing on external events and the social context to help them understand a given situation. Because of this tendency, they are more oriented toward perspective-taking and understanding the behaviors of others. This propensity helps them to better read other people. In fact, in an earlier study, researchers found that in situations where lower-class individuals had control over others, they tended to ignore context just as upper-class individuals are prone to do (Kraus, Piff, & Keltner, 2009). This suggests that having control and hence power over situations translates into less attention to context and to others and helps to explain the lower levels of empathy for some individuals of upper-class backgrounds.

Empathy is not the only prosocial behavior that is lower in individuals from higher social classes. Based on a review of studies on social class rank, Kraus, Piff and Keltner (2011) identified the relationship between class rank and psychological orientations and behaviors. They posit that people of low social rank have a greater understanding of the social environment and context and are other-oriented and prosocial, whereas people of high social rank attend more to individual dispositions than context, are self-oriented, and demonstrate more disengaged and selfish behaviors. Although not every person of higher social class has power, and not every person with power is of higher social class, in most cases the two go hand in hand. How, then, does this profile of socially higher ranked people being less prosocial fit with the previous findings that those in power with a prosocial orientation have higher empathic accuracy? We might conclude that it is less likely for those of higher social rank to engage in prosocial behaviors, but when they do, they are very good at being empathic.

It may not seem surprising to you that with higher social rank and power, people are less likely to be empathic. Empathy requires attention to others, and when a person is in a powerful position of control, what others of lower rank think or feel does not matter, since they have no power to make any difference in the current situation. But what about people who are not in power, but grab any authority they can get and in those roles, lack empathy? It turns out that just believing that social hierarchies are good and that some groups are naturally superior to others is enough to impact empathic accuracy (Sherman, Lerner, Renshon, Ma-Kellams, & Joel, 2015). The brain activity of individuals who believe in social dominance of one group over others was lower in response to perceiving pain in others (Chiao, Mathur, Harada, & Lipke, 2009). It may be that if one is predisposed to think in terms of group identities rather than individual traits, and also believe that inequalities between groups are a given part of our social system, then tuning into others is not a skill that will be developed or thought to be important. Power seems to act as a mediator of empathy and other prosocial behaviors. If people in power have an inclination toward being empathic, then they are successful at creating prosocial outcomes. However, since those in power tend to lack incentive to understand those with less power and tend not to attend to context, they are less likely to be empathic. The challenge then is in finding ways to encourage those with power to be interested in the perspectives of others, particularly those over whom they have power. Although this is not an easy task, we address this challenge at the end of this chapter in a discussion of the malleability of empathy.

Genocide, Apartheid, and Slavery

Otherness seems to be at the foundation of most barriers to empathy. But is the impact of ingroup bias and viewing the world as "us" versus "them" enough to explain horrific acts of organized violence? Otherness certainly plays a part, but so does how we regard other people.

First and foremost is whether we consider another person to be "fully human" (Fiske, 2009, p. 32) and consider the person's inner life and thoughts when interacting with him or her (Harris & Fiske, 2011). Thus, if we consider others to be fully human, we can experience empathy for them. However, if we do not view them as fully human, the empathic process will likely be bypassed. Neurological data supports these points. When viewing pictures of different individuals who were identified in previous research as belonging to groups that elicit disgust (such as drug addicts, homeless persons), participants did not have significant activation in the medial prefrontal cortex (mPFC) brain region, which is where we would find mentalizing and cognitive processing, but did experience neural activity in the amygdala and insula, areas linked more to affective response (Harris & Fiske, 2006). The researchers note that the neural differences when viewing outgroups that are dehumanized allow for a form of cognitive distancing.

Participants did not engage fully the part of the brain that corresponds to thinking about others (the mPFC brain region) when viewing the out groups compared to seeing pictures of those who belong to groups that evoke pity (such as elderly people) or pride (such as Olympic athletes). The authors conclude that experiencing mental distancing from others who evoke disgust may contribute to the ability to commit atrocities. When we apply these neurological findings to what we know about empathy, it appears that affective stimuli are taken in when viewing all groups, but then not processed through cognitive means such as self-other awareness and perspective-taking for certain groups. Although this contributes to a person not connecting with another on a personal level, how might it proceed to such atrocities as genocide, mass murder, or acts of terrorism?

Staub (2015) makes a compelling argument that there are two contextual conditions that precipitate such violence. The first predictor is that a society is in a state of major difficulty, such as political upheaval, economic depression, or significant social change in a relatively short period of time, and the second predictor is the existence of a long-standing, seemingly intractable conflict with another group. He argues that these conditions trigger the psychological need for security, safety, control, and an understanding of the world. When these psychological needs are not met, attachment to one's own group or a group that holds an ideology that promises solutions to the chaos becomes attractive and comforting. If one's own group should move towards violence to control other groups, members are connected to their group for security and safety and already primed to see the other group as unlike them due to the long-standing historical divisions. This combination of environmental pressures (such as political upheaval or economic instability) with group divisions can be the ingredients that lead to violence.

Given the human tendency to have preferential bias for ingroup members and have lower empathic connections with outgroup members, coupled with the external conditions and long-standing group divisions that Staub (2015) cites, the foundation for committing atrocities can be set. The history of humanity includes numerous efforts by one group to dominate other groups and even completely annihilate them. Social psychologist Peter Glick (2005, 2008) has done extensive research on intergroup relations and the breakdown that results in genocide. His work reflects that of Staub's. He describes the phenomenon of "ideological scapegoating," which involves an increase in the social construction of stereotypes to explain why situations are the way they are and places blame for social problems on the identified scapegoated group. Often underlying such attitudes are misunderstandings or oversimplifications of social, political, or economic conditions that may be too complex to comprehend. Seeking answers, people are easily swayed by the blaming of others, especially others who are different and perceived as less than human. In addition, there are often seeds of distrust or long-standing beliefs about the other group that can stretch back generations, centuries, even millennia, which surface in troubling times (Glick & Paluck, 2013). Blaming one group for the problems of a larger society is the form of scapegoating that Glick (2008) has identified in key historical events such as the Holocaust and the Rwandan genocide. The scapegoated group is not only different, but in these cases where the conflict escalated, the other group was seen as so different that they were not seen as part of the other group's humanity. When others become inhuman objects, there is no mirroring of the self, and no perspective-taking.

Studying the history of genocide and hate from the perspective of groups competing for resources and power, Robbins and DiDomenica (2013) echo the analyses above and consider empathy the antidote. But they warn that because fear of others activates primitive survival mechanisms, the cognitive processing of empathy can be easily manipulated:

> Various situational factors involving conflict with an *out-group* such as disputed territory, present state of war, or previous history of war or violence, and limited resources can easily be woven by leaders into a compelling story to alarm the primal fears of their followers related to survival and reproductive fitness. The occurrence of a present crisis and the identification of a responsible *out-group* are all that is needed to evoke these primal repto-mammalian fears and convince the thinking neocortical mind that the annihilation of the out-group is necessary or, at least, create an indifference to and lack of empathy towards the out-group. (p. 24)

Such can be the case in the political realm, although not in such an extreme way as promotion of genocide. When politicians make stereotypical generalizations about groups with the aim of stirring fear (as when Donald Trump, for example, referred to undocumented immigrants as "criminals, drug dealers, and rapists" in the speech in which he announced his run for president [Leibovich, 2015]) it can have the effect of pitting groups against each other. Framing entire groups as others to be feared is a step in the dehumanizing process and obstructs any possibility of empathic insight. Knowing this can, however, present opportunities to enhance empathic abilities. The components of social empathy, taking steps to understand history and context while engaging in macro perspective-taking, are the antidotes and can bring out empathy on the larger societal stage.

Stress as a Barrier to Empathy

One last barrier to empathy is important to mention—namely, stress—although it is not typically seen as a direct block to our brains engaging in empathic processing. The literature on empathic brain functioning in relation to stress-related brain functioning is scant, although there is overlap in terms of components such as emotion regulation. In his exhaustive book on stress and stress-related diseases, Sapolsky (2004) provides a thorough discussion of neural processes and how stress impacts the healthy functioning of our brains, but he does not specifically mention empathy. However, the brain activities that are impacted by stress include those that are critical to engaging in empathic insight.

Biologically, we are designed to handle stressful events through a change in our physiological state (Arnsten, 2009; Gouin, Hantsoo, & Kiecolt-Glaser, 2011; Sapolsky, 2004). Faced with a stressor, such as a threat to our survival, our amygdala activates the hypothalamus, which triggers the release of high levels of noradrenaline dopamine, which send messages for the release of more glucose, proteins, and fats to power us with enough energy to respond and hence survive. The biological delivery of these resources can be felt through an increased heart rate, faster breathing, and a heightened sense of alertness to stimuli in what some of us may have experienced as an "adrenaline rush." In order to focus all the body's energy on the physical fight or flight response, the prefrontal cortex region (PFC) of the brain is put on hold (as are other nonemergency related functions such as digestion, reproduction, growth, and immune system processes) because at the moment there is no need for these higher-level functions. Instead the most pressing need is to focus all energy on the immediate stressor. In fact, the amygdala's function is strengthened, making one even more alert to affective stimuli. This process is highly functional because it produces the energy needed to respond immediately in what is often referred to as "fight-or-flight response" to avoid imminent danger.

There is some disagreement as to whether the fight or flight response is the only basic response to stress, particularly for women. Taylor (2002, 2006) posits that faced with threat to one's offspring, women respond to stress in a "tend and befriend" process. Tending is the nurturance and protection of offspring and befriending is the creation and maintenance of social support, usually other women who gather to aid in the protection process. One theory put forth is that with birth and nurturance, there is an increase in levels of oxytocin (Taylor & Master, 2010), and as noted in chapter 2, oxytocin may enhance empathic abilities—hence, women's tendency for a "tend and befriend" response rather than a fight or flight response, at least in regard to offspring.

The problem is that these evolutionary biological processes for enhancing survival of the species are not meant to address repeated exposure to stressors or living with long-term stress, which is what we typically experience today, not the life-threatening emergency of a saber-toothed tiger chasing us. Rather, we face prolonged stresses such as working for a difficult boss, or trying to make ends meet on a small salary, or arguing with family members, or any number of issues that keep us awake at night. The body does not recognize this kind of stress as different from the life-threatening version, which is a problem, since frequent activation of the stress response, particularly in early life development (Lupien, McEwen, Gunnar, & Heim, 2009; National Scientific Council on the Developing Child, 2014), can cause tremendous harm—increased blood pressure, suppression of the immune system, imbalances in neurochemicals that may contribute to the development of psychiatric disorders, disruption to the metabolic system, which can impede development in children and lead to diabetes as they age, and increases in lipid levels, which can lead to atherosclerosis (Taylor, 2010). Even the advantages of oxytocin may be compromised and even detrimental when longer-lasting and released repeatedly (Taylor & Master, 2010). The list of physical outcomes that can be impacted by stress is quite troubling. Moreover, as all these stress responses are going on in the body, cognitive processing, which includes the key empathy components of self-other awareness, perspective-taking, and emotion regulation, is impaired. "During stress, orchestration of the brain's response patterns switches from slow, thoughtful PFC regulation to the reflexive and rapid emotional responses of the amygdala and related subcortical structures" (Arnsten, 2009, p. 411).

Human beings are holistic systems, and when one part of the system is impacted so too are others. This can be positive, as in the case of empathy: We experience unconscious physiological stimuli that then trigger a mental process of interpreting what those stimuli might mean. But with stress that process is interrupted, and when this interruption is repeated or extended over time, it may lead to impairment of our cognitive processing. Buruck, Wendsche, Melzer, Strobel, and Dörfel (2014) provide experimental data on the relationship between stress and empathy. In their study, one group of participants experienced stressful tasks that included developing and performing a speech in front of trained evaluators in front of cameras while a comparison group was asked to talk about a holiday trip in an empty room without any evaluation. Following the tasks, the groups were compared on their ability to assess pain in others. Measuring heart rates and using self-reports to assess physiological states, the experimenters found that the stressed participants rated others' pain lower than did the participants in the control group. They also looked at emotion regulation skills, and found that higher levels of acceptance or tolerance of negative emotions was related to lower rating of pain in others. The researchers suggest the ability to regulate one's emotions may help to keep the individual from becoming distressed, which can be helpful in taking empathic action, as when health-care workers treat patients in pain. But there can also be a dysfunctional side to tolerance or acceptance of others' pain, which is manifest as a lack of feeling or numbness to others' pain. The researchers are careful to point out that this was an experiment inducing acute stress, which may be treated differently than chronic stress. We may be able to regulate our emotions more easily for a specific incident of stress, but facing long-term continuing stress may have a different outcome in terms of our ability to regulate our emotions.

Using the same stress inducers as in Buruck et al. (2014), which are described above, Tomova, von Dawans, Heinrichs, Silani, and Lamm (2014) found that men responded with self-focus and increased fight-or-flight response behaviors, while women were able to overcome self-focus and show an increase in social interaction skills that reflect the tend-and-befriend response. In a recent study on short-term induced stress, participants reported higher levels of affective empathic responses, but there did not seem to be any impact on cognitive empathy (Wolf, Schulte, Drimella, Hamacher-Dang, Knoch, & Dziobek, 2015).

Together these studies suggest that incidents of stress may heighten affective arousal, which, if combined with emotion regulation, may lead to empathic concern, as well as suggesting that this outcome is more likely for women. For the most part though, incidents of acute stress do not affect cognitive aspects of empathic processing. Thus, at best, stress may help in short-term affective attention, but repeated or long-term exposure to stress has the potential to compromise the cognitive processes of empathy. If our stress response was only needed to occasionally respond to an immediate threat, then it is likely that empathy would not be adversely affected, and might even be triggered. However, what about the impact on empathy of stressors that are long-lasting and may be a condition of childhood such as poverty?

The key contributors to stress are loss of control and a lack of predictability (Sapolsky, 2004). Living in poverty means constantly lacking both control and predictability. Thus, it is not surprising to find that poverty increases stress-related diseases: "If you want to increase the odds of living a long and healthy life, don't be poor. Poverty is associated with increased risks of cardiovascular disease, respiratory disease, ulcers, rheumatoid disorders, psychiatric diseases, and a number of types of cancer, just to name a few" (Sapolsky, 2004, p. 366). Poverty also impacts neural activity. Adults from low socioeconomic backgrounds demonstrate less connectivity between the anterior cingulate cortex (ACC) and the orbitofrontal cortex (OFC) (Gianaros et al., 2011), regions associated with affective arousal and emotion regulation. Growing up in poverty results in elevated levels of chronic stress and impaired working memory (Evans & Schamberg, 2009), an executive function that occurs in the prefrontal cortex (PFC). These findings suggest that a lifetime of poverty negatively impacts brain regions associated with empathy. Although this is discouraging, given the structural embeddedness of poverty for a significant portion of our population, recent research is finding that the skill of emotion regulation can protect children from having their working memory impaired, although not from the physiological stresses of poverty (Evans & Fuller-Rowell, 2013). Even though the research does not address empathy, we know that emotion regulation is an important part of empathy, and given that it can enhance functions in the PFC region of the brain for children experiencing long-term stress from living in poverty, developing emotion regulation may be both an antidote to some of the debilitating effects of poverty and a pathway to enhanced empathy even when living under conditions of chronic stress. In fact, we now know that the brain can develop and change throughout life. Our brains have the property of *neuroplasticity*, which means that brain structure and patterns of activity of the neural pathways in the brain can change (Davidson & Begley, 2012), and thus training that focuses on changes in the structure and function of the brain can address even the effects of chronic stress (Davdison & McEwen, 2012). Neuroplasticity means that empathy can be developed and enhanced, even if events in life have adversely impacted the functioning of the brain.

THE GOOD NEWS—THE MALLEABILITY OF EMPATHY

Although we are hard-wired to mirror, which can then lead to empathic feelings, there are barriers to that resonance. Some of these barriers may be inherited and have to do with species survival, but most barriers seem to be cognitively developed, albeit perhaps on an unconscious level at a young age. To the extent that our beliefs influence our mentalized images, self-other awareness, perspective-taking, and our ability to regulate our emotions, then one key target of intervention would be people's attitudes toward others, especially attitudes toward those whom they regard as different. There are numerous ways to influence or change people's attitudes; the challenge is in finding the best and strongest. Experiential learning that taps into one's empathic neural system seems to be the most effective way to change one's feelings toward those who are perceived as different. The shift to seeing others not as different but as similar seems to be the strongest way to influence empathic resonance or insight. Moreover, the relationship is circular and mutually reinforcing: Increased empathic resonance with others induces increased understanding of others, and increased understanding of others seems to induce greater empathy for others.

Thus, perhaps the starting point is increasing empathy, because that opens one up emotionally to understanding, and not just intellectually. It suggests a stronger way of learning.

We know that attitudes toward stigmatized groups or outgroup members are very difficult to change. There are a few possible approaches, such as providing positive information about other groups including historical perspective. Information, though, may not be impactful in an emotional way. Personal experience can be powerful, but difficult to arrange across different groups. This leaves perspective-taking (PT) on the individual level as a good place to start.

In a now classic study, Batson et al. (1997) tested whether invoking empathy for a stigmatized outgroup member might have an impact on empathy for the overall group. They found that an increase in empathy for individuals from an outgroup extended to the outgroup as a whole. In another set of experiments, Galinsky and Moskowitz (2000) found that perspective-taking helped to increase self-other overlap and foster a feeling of connection to previously stereotyped groups, thereby diminishing the expression of bias.

The impact of PT might depend on whether we can actually imagine ourselves in the other's situation. Chambers and Davis (2012), over several studies, found participants with similar prior experiences and an ability to imagine being in that situation again were more empathic than both those without prior experience and even those with prior experience if they could not imagine being in the situation again. They offer the concept of *ease of self-simulation* (ESS), or rapid decision-making about how to feel and whether to help based on ease of imagining oneself in the situation of another, as key. "The 'easier' it feels to imagine the self in the target's position, the more empathy we are likely to feel and the more help we are to offer" (Davis, 2015, p. 302). One challenge in promoting PT is the differential due to power. DeTurk (2001) suggests members of marginalized groups have the potential to better understand the social order because they must be "bilingual" or "bicultural" to navigate their own group and that of those in dominant power positions. Even for outsiders, the dominant culture is easily experienced, since it pervades most institutions. To survive, subordinate group members need to understand the dominant culture and move safely within it, and such understanding is especially important as a way to experience success (social mobility, for example) within it. However, dominant group members do not have experience with subordinate groups' cultures and typically have no need to negotiate their worlds. Thus, the skills needed to be empathically attuned to others are less necessary for survival for dominant group members compared to subordinate group members. Finding ways to persuade those from dominant cultures to engage in PT of nondominant group members is a challenge and requires creative ways to tap into the ease of self-simulation.

Recent research has begun the exploration of using fMRI technology to train people to use neurofeedback to change the patterns of interactions in their brain circuitry in response to emotional stimuli, particularly pain (Yao et al. 2016). Participants were trained in techniques for neurofeedback, and through the training, brain patterns of self-regulation were improved as observed in real time through fMRIs. The neurofeedback process was used to enhance emotion regulation and resulted in stronger empathic responses. The alterations in brain activity were evident when reexamined two days later. While this is preliminary research in this area, it suggests that there may be significant potential in using brain imaging technology in real time to teach neurofeedback techniques in emotion regulation to help improve emotional responses, including empathy. This example of altering brain activity through willful exercise demonstrates the possibility for changing neural pathways.

The malleability of neural pathways opens the possibility of reworking brain activity to enhance empathy. Techniques that reroute neural reactions, whether through behavioral training or neurofeedback, benefit from using the empathy components to identify specific behavior areas, such as using meditation to promote emotion regulation or reading historical books to understand other culture's context. Tools for training can be focused on each component, and have the result of overcoming barriers and enhancing empathy interpersonally, as well as within and between groups. Overall, empathy training programs do seem to encourage increased levels of empathy, but clarity on the mechanisms that make this happen still requires additional research (Teding van Berkhout & Malouff, 2016).

Linking Interpersonal and Social Empathy

UP TO THIS POINT IN THE BOOK, although we have introduced the distinction between interpersonal empathy and social empathy, we have for the most part addressed the overall concept of empathy. We noted where there might be differences between the two, but we have not focused on how these two forms of empathy are related. In this chapter, we present the theoretical foundation for how interpersonal and social empathy are connected and share findings from a study looking at levels of interpersonal empathy and social empathy and how they might be related. Because each perspective of empathy can have a different focus and outcome for action, it is helpful to examine individual empathic focus and societal empathic focus separately.

The development of social empathy and how it relates to interpersonal empathy are emerging areas of research that we have begun to explore, and hope others will follow. The conceptual development of the distinction between the two areas of empathy is based on our professional practice as well as recent research. The origin of the distinction came about as a result of a number of questions that we have faced in the classroom and while working with different individuals, groups, and communities. The overarching question is: How do we enhance people's capacity to care about others? In the work and teaching we do, training for interpersonal empathy is a challenge, but not a mystery. We have tools to teach interpersonal empathy (Gerdes, Segal, Jackson, & Mullins, 2011). However, teaching social empathy seems to be more difficult. How do we cultivate the type of empathic reactions that people demonstrate toward friends and family members in their responses to groups who differ from them, particularly groups that have historically been the focus of prejudice and oppression? And even more challenging, how do we get that empathic insight to influence and shape the public policies and programs that make up our social welfare system in this country? These questions are the genesis of conceptualizing and researching social empathy.

In this chapter, we are taking a slightly different approach to probe the relationship between interpersonal empathy and social empathy in that we are presenting original research findings. This is a new area of study, and there is little empirical work done on it thus far. There is, however, theoretical work that supports our research, and we will start with that information, before moving onto our research.

APPLYING WHAT WE KNOW ABOUT EMPATHY TO SOCIAL LIVING

We have already noted that survival and genetic reproduction are best accomplished through group living that relies on empathic behaviors among group members (Carter, Harris, & Porges, 2011; deWaal, 2009; Hoffman, 2000; Keltner, 2010). Because of the evolutionary imperatives of survival and reproduction, people's empathic feelings are stronger for those who will help to ensure successful survival and reproduction. And those most likely to ensure our survival have been others who look, think, and act similarly, particularly in terms of race, gender, age, ability, political identification, and social class (Brown, Bradley, & Lang, 2006; Chiao & Mathur, 2010; Xu, Zuo, Wang, & Han, 2009). Unfortunately, our tribal instinct, coupled with our relative difficulty in enacting empathy for people who are different from us, often results in a tendency toward "us versus them" attitudes and behaviors (Stürmer & Snyder, 2010), and in most modern-day instances, these are counterproductive.

The human tendency to be less empathic and more prejudiced toward people who are different presents a major obstacle for social cooperation and facilitating social well-being. How can we understand the needs of *others* if we maintain the empathic distance that has come with our historical evolution? How can we close the empathy gap between *ingroup* and *outgroup* membership? How can we encourage voters and policymakers to extend resources and services to people who are different from them? One answer to this problem is to facilitate the development of *social empathy*. Whereas interpersonal empathy is the ability to feel and understand the emotions of others, typically individuals, social empathy requires the application of empathic insights to larger social groups and conditions (Segal, 2014). Social empathy is "the ability to understand people by perceiving or experiencing their life situations and as a result gain insight into structural inequalities and disparities" (Segal, 2011, pp. 266–267).

We know that interpersonal empathy is considered a key aspect of pro-social development. What is less defined and understood is the relationship of interpersonal empathy to understanding larger social systems, which is the domain of social empathy. Rifkin (2009) considers the ability to see ourselves in others as involving a recognition that each person is unique and deserving of equal consideration in the arena of shared social life. He points out that this view is behind our principle that all people have "inalienable rights," that is, those human rights that cannot be taken away, such as life, liberty, and the pursuit of happiness (which are explicitly spelled out in the United States' Declaration of Independence). That is why Rifkin calls empathy the "soul of democracy" (p. 161). He goes on to point out that the evolution of empathy has gone hand in hand with the evolution of democracy and that conversely, where there is less empathy in a culture, there is less democratic process and more totalitarian governing. Michael Morrell (2010) also links empathy and democracy and argues for deeper empathic insights into social relations and systems in order to enhance democratic processes and social tolerance. "Human history gives ample evidence that majorities are much more likely to act in a way that ignores or marginalizes minorities, even after reflection. Requiring that deliberative reflection include empathy will make it more likely that majorities are conscious of how their actions affect minorities" (p. 175). Deliberative reflection calls for thinking about what the possible impact of our policy decisions may have on all, but especially those who are less dominant politically, socially and economically.

Broader empathic understanding can enhance global understanding. By using social empathy skills, people gain insight into their place among others, which can foster a sense of empowerment that they can have an impact on the outside world (Wagaman, 2011). With increased social engagement, a sense of community is promoted and people are more likely to protect public interests (Putnam, 1993). Overall, social empathy can contribute to improved democratic processes, increased global understanding, and greater empowerment to engage in social change.

CONTEXT AND THE GAP BETWEEN INTERPERSONAL
EMPATHY AND SOCIAL EMPATHY

Although levels of empathy can vary, the highest levels of empathy are linked to understanding context and situation (Walter, 2012). Recall the experiment described in chapter 2, in which the contexts in which teacups were observed resulted in different brain activations. To fully develop one's interpersonal empathic abilities, it is necessary to "go beyond what is directly available" such as facial expressions and actions and include interpretation of the context in which these occur (Zahavi, 2012, p. 81). Lack of attention to context can lead to erroneous interpretations and limit empathic insights (Singer & Lamm, 2009). For example, suppose that you are shown a picture of needles inserted into a foot. At first the picture might evoke pain and discomfort within you and lead you to feel concern for the welfare of the person in the image and possibly your own feelings of discomfort or pain. But if you are told that what you are seeing is an acupuncture procedure and that it is being used to decrease pain affecting the person's foot, you are more likely to experience empathy rather than discomfort or pain. Once you are exposed to the image within a particular context, you can cognitively process the situation and avert the initial sense of discomfort or distress that you might feel. This example was put to the test with fMRI (Lamm, Nusbaum, Meltzoff, & Decety, 2007). Participants were shown pictures of hands being injected by a needle. One set had no accompanying explanation, while another included an introductory explanation that this was a biopsy needle and that the hand was anesthetized, so there was no feeling of pain. Both pictures elicited an automatic response to pain in brain activity, but differed in that for the pictures with the anesthetized hand, there was modulation by brain activity in regions of the temporo-parietal junction, which is involved in self-other awareness and mentalizing. The researchers suggest that in the case of knowing that the hand was numb and not feeling pain, the cognitive processing that regulated the pain matrix in the brain was activated. This research demonstrates that we are likely to activate cognitive processes to balance our own affective response to seeing another's pain, and knowing the contextual circumstances around that pain is one way to do so. Thus, can understanding of social context of different populations and groups translate into changed cognitive processing and in turn elevate empathic feelings?

The field of neuroscience, while leading us in understanding the neural aspects of empathy in our brains, acknowledges that broader insight into social context and cultural differences is important as well. Leading cognitive and social neuroscientists agree that "empathy is influenced by social context" (Decety, 2015, p. 4) and that neuroscience needs to consider the complexity of empathy within the context of the social environment (Zaki & Ochsner, 2012). We need ways to look at empathy cross-culturally in naturally occurring settings so we can better analyze "the variety of cultural frameworks, social situations, and political-economic conditions that tend to either suppress and inhibit basic empathy or amplify it into a frequent and reliable means of social knowing" (Hollan, 2012, p. 76). Activating the social empathy component of contextual understanding can contribute to a deeper level of insight and then can be enhanced by macro self-other awareness and perspective-taking.

MACRO SELF-OTHER AWARENESS AND PERSPECTIVE-TAKING

We know the importance of self-other awareness and perspective-taking for interpersonal empathy. These are the cognitive skills that help us to understand the experiences of others. So how might these skills differ in a broader social context? In defining social intelligence, Daniel Goleman includes the ability of what he refers to as *social awareness*, which combines empathy with knowing how the social world works (2006). Goleman's concept of social awareness describes processes we go through all the time when we interact with others. That process involves an array of what he describes as social calculations. For example, when a teacher enters her classroom, she consciously and unconsciously takes in the surroundings and the students. A lot of neural activity is going on for the teacher; she is engaged in social awareness. Goleman primarily applies this skill to interpersonal relations. However, if applied more broadly to larger social groups, it would more closely reflect what we mean by macro self-other awareness and perspective-taking. These skills include a level of social awareness that allows us to take in the perspective of members of groups who are very different from us while attending to context, including historical events and social structures. All too often we interpret behaviors of people in other cultures based on what we expect of our own culture, without knowledge and understanding of the different culture and structures of their society.

For example, ten years after the invasion of Iraq, analysis of what actually happened in the years following the engagement of American troops (Dodge, 2013) closely mirrors the descriptions by Pinker (2011) of what leads to violent states based on thousands of years of history, as discussed in chapter 3. Violence takes hold where there is a lack of functioning government. Removing a functioning but brutal government improves social well-being if it is replaced by an alternative supportive governing system; social well-being is not served by swapping one totalitarian government for another. Furthermore, historical in-fighting between groups, or long-standing feuds, also contribute to the ingredients that can lead to an environment for dehumanized violence (as discussed in chapter 4). Unfortunately in Iraq, a destroyed government followed by no controlling alternative government, coupled with the long-standing animosity between cultural groups, contributed key ingredients for civil war and dehumanized violence. This outcome might have been predicted from the study of historical events as chronicled by the analyses of Pinker (2011) and Staub (2015). Was a calculation of what might happen after removing the existing governing control in light of the long-standing animosity between population groups missing from the planning prior to the invasion of Iraq? Were those making the decisions basing their plans on what people familiar with a democracy like the United States might want, not what would best fit the indigenous population? Might they have suffered from what we also know about lower levels of empathy in those with power (as discussed in chapter 4)? Of course we do not know what exactly went into the planning; maybe there were other factors that necessitated taking known risks. However, placing ourselves in the context of that region's history and taking the perspective of those who live there might have enabled us to foresee some of the problems, such as the deep level of animosity between groups. The need for social empathy before engaging in such powerful acts is crucial and can lead to different outcomes.

As discussed in chapter 4, we find that when empathy is induced for members of stigmatized groups, feelings towards the group as a whole are improved (Batson et al., 1997). And we know that perspective-taking is a key component of interpersonal empathy and can diminish expressions of racial bias (Todd, Bodenhausen, Richeson, & Galinsky, 2011), as well as reduce racial disparities in pain treatment (Drwecki, Moore, Ward, & Prkachin, 2011). Such macro perspective-taking, coupled with analyses of historical human events, suggest that gaining information through the eyes of others who are different on a societal level might lead to deeper understanding of social conditions in which those others live. And with a deeper understanding, we can frame actions not only according to our own worldview, but also in terms of a broad spectrum of perspectives. This process of macro self-other awareness and perspective-taking is the contribution of social empathy.

THE RESEARCH WE CONDUCTED

Conceptually, we can see that interpersonal empathy and social empathy are connected, in that both involve many of the same neural actions. But can we see how these two forms of empathy are connected in people, and if so, how? Specifically, we wondered if people with high levels of social empathy also have high levels of interpersonal empathy, and conversely, if people with low levels of interpersonal empathy also have low levels of social empathy? We were also interested in finding out whether high levels of interpersonal empathy might be linked to social empathy in such a way that social empathy is built on a foundation of interpersonal empathy. These questions guided our research.

We approached the research hypothesizing that participants would fall into three groups (low, medium, high) based on their self-reported levels of interpersonal empathy (IE) and social empathy (SE). We predicted that participants with high levels of social empathy are more likely to have high levels of interpersonal empathy, but we were not sure whether having a high level of interpersonal empathy necessarily meant there would be a high level of social empathy. We also looked at what the impact of ethnicity, gender, and socioeconomic status might be on empathy levels. Additional details of the research and statistical analyses used can be found in appendix A.

Participants

We analyzed the self-report data of 450 undergraduate college students who ranged in age from 18 to 61 years, with an average age of 23. Two-thirds of the participants were female, and one-third were male. Of those who reported their ethnicity, a little over half identified as Caucasian, 16 percent as Latino, 8 percent as Asian, 8 percent as Middle Eastern, 8 percent as multiracial, 5 percent as African American, and almost 2 percent as American Indian. The participants identified more than 40 different academic areas of primary study, with the five largest groups identifying their major as criminal justice, social work, engineering, psychology, and business. Twenty-eight percent of the sample reported their family of origin socioeconomic status as poor or working class; 42 percent of the participants reported their family of origin socioeconomic status as middle class, and 26 percent reported as upper class.

Measures

Data were collected on items from the Empathy Assessment Index (EAI) and the Social Empathy Index (SEI), which are explained in detail in the next chapter. Through statistical analyses based on the findings of an exploratory factor analysis, a technique used to identify relationships between variables, the most salient items reflecting the components of interpersonal and social empathy were used for comparison. The fourteen items that were statistically identified and thus stood out are listed in box 5.1.

Participants were asked to rate how closely the items reflected their feelings or beliefs on a 6-point Likert-type scale, which allows for participants to rank items from a low of never (1) to a high of always (6). Higher scores indicate higher levels of self-reported interpersonal empathy and social empathy.

Results

As we hypothesized, the participants did fall into three categories (low, medium, and high) for both interpersonal empathy (IE) and social empathy (SE). We had expected that higher levels of social empathy would be correlated with higher levels of interpersonal empathy. Table 5.1, which shows the 3 × 3 cross-tabulation of the categories, supports this expectation. The most populated cells in the table fall along the diagonal, such that 23.5 percent of the sample displays low IE/low SE, 25.3 percent are medium IE/medium SE, and 16 percent are high IE/high SE. Those three matched

BOX 5.1   INTERPERSONAL AND SOCIAL EMPATHY ITEMS
FOLLOWING EXPLORATORY FACTOR ANALYSIS

When I see someone receive a gift that makes them happy, I feel happy myself.

When I am with someone who gets sad news, I feel sad for a moment too.

Hearing laughter makes me smile

I can consider my point of view and another person's point of view at the same time.

When I see a person experiencing a strong emotion, I can accurately assess what that person is feeling.

I can tell the difference between someone else's feelings and my own.

I am aware of what other people think of me.

I am aware of other people's emotions.

I can explain to others how I am feeling.

I take action to help others even if it does not personally benefit me.

I am comfortable helping a person of a different race or ethnicity than my own.

I feel it is important to understand the political perspectives of people I don't agree with.

I believe that people who face discrimination have added stress that negatively impacts their lives.

I believe government should protect the rights of minorities.

categories reflected almost two-thirds of the participants. And, the pattern followed what we would expect—namely, that those low in IE were also low in SE, those in the middle group of IE were also in the middle of SE, and those with high IE were also high in SE. Unmatched levels of empathy were much less common. Only 1.3 percent of the participants were classified as high IE and low SE, while 4.5 percent were classified as low IE and high SE.

We also considered whether levels of social empathy might relate to levels of interpersonal empathy. The details of the statistical analyses are outlined in appendix A. What we found was that the level of social empathy was predicted by the level of interpersonal empathy—that is, those with high levels of social empathy were vastly more likely to also have high levels of

TABLE 5.1   Groupings by Level of Interpersonal
and Social Empathy

		INTERPERSONAL EMPATHY		
		LOW	MED	HIGH
Social empathy	Low	23.5%	8.2%	1.3%
	Med	4.7%	25.3%	4.2%
	High	4.5%	12.2%	16.0%

interpersonal empathy. Our analyses of gender, ethnic, and socioeconomic status revealed some interesting findings. Generally, the largest nondominant group in our study, Latinos, had higher levels of social empathy than did participants who identified being Caucasian.

What Do the Results Suggest?

It appears likely that the level of a person's social empathy corresponds to his or her level of interpersonal empathy since those with high SE scores also had high IE scores. Conceptually, this relationship makes sense. The foundation for strong SE would be expected to include good IE skills. High IE includes abilities such as the cognitive processing of affective responses and awareness of the feelings of others, which are critical to empathic insight at any level, whether micro or macro. This relationship suggests that in order to increase people's social empathic abilities, a foundation of strong interpersonal empathy skills is beneficial. Here, then, is a starting place for cultivating social empathy—training people to have strong interpersonal empathy skills upon which they can build the macro perspective-taking skills of social empathy.

There were some statistically significant differences for the Latino participants. The odds of a Latino participant falling into both the higher and medium SE categories were substantially higher than for white participants. Although there were greater numbers of white participants compared to Latino participants (236 versus 73), which makes drawing conclusions difficult, these differences are worth noting for future research. Given the outgroup status of Latinos in our geographic community, it is possible that their position as outsider promotes greater contextual understanding and macro perspective-taking. That is, being outside the dominant culture may require dual understandings, that of your own culture and that of the larger dominant culture. This is an ability that would not be as critical to day-to-day functioning for white participants and could be responsible for the differences in social empathy scores. This finding reflects DeTurk's (2001) point, discussed at the end of chapter 4, that marginalized groups need to be "bicultural" and navigate through both the dominant culture and their own. Having a higher level of social empathy would help one do that. The findings from this research confirm that with stronger capacities for interpersonal empathy, the foundation is set for increasing social empathy.

FOR THE FUTURE

Although we hope to see much more research on the relationship between interpersonal empathy and social empathy, our findings provide a starting point, which is to build interpersonal empathy. A strong foundation of interpersonal empathy coupled with abilities in contextual understanding and macro perspective-taking, the key elements of social empathy, provides a promising pathway to infusing greater socially empathic insights into group relationships and public policies. Socially empathic group relationships and public policies in turn promote enhanced social well-being. To be able to assess whether we are successfully raising people's levels of both interpersonal and social empathy it is helpful to have instruments to measure these abilities. The next chapter presents three instruments, with background information on the development of these instruments, which can be used to measure interpersonal and social empathy.

6

Tools for Measuring and Assessing Empathy

ONE GOAL IN WRITING THIS BOOK was to share the instruments we developed for measuring empathy. However, before we could introduce the instruments, we needed to explain what is meant by the term *empathy* and how it fits with human behavior and larger social systems. Recent neuroscience findings that have traced the brain activity related to empathic thinking and feeling also needed to be discussed. Admittedly, there has been a lot to say, so it is only now in chapter 6 that we are finally sharing the instruments. Although you may be feeling "it's about time," we think the instruments can be more effective in research and training after being given the prior information.

Before measuring something, we need to know what it is and what it looks like. That was where we started with empathy. That meant defining it first as a concept; only then can we measure it as an observable behavior. Definitions and ways to observe empathy vary and consequently there have been significant differences in how empathy has been conceptualized and hence measured (Gerdes, Segal, & Lietz, 2010; Gerdes, Lietz, & Segal, 2011). That is why we started this book with information on the history of definitions of empathy and where we are today. Recall that the major views of empathy split between the sharing of feelings between people, or what is often referred to as emotional empathy, or the imagining of being in another's place, which is what we would consider to be mentalizing and perspective-taking. Additionally, much of the literature on empathy made a distinction between emotional empathy and affective empathy. The first view posits that we share emotional feelings when we see a person's actions. The second suggests that we react to seeing another person's behaviors in a way that can be devoid of emotions. Today, we consider empathy to include all of those aspects—the reaction to observed behaviors, the sharing of feelings, and the taking the role of another—along with emotion regulation, which is often not addressed. Thanks to neuroscientific brain imaging and social cognitive psychology, we can identify several components that come together as empathy, or what we have referred to as the full scope of empathy. Once we were satisfied that we had a definition of empathy that reflected the latest research from cognitive and social neuroscience, we wanted to identify the best ways to develop those components and enhance people's overall empathy.

We researched all the ways that empathy had been measured since the concept came into use, and discovered that the most common way of measuring empathy between adults was through the use of self-reports. However, all the self-report instruments reflected what we knew about empathy prior to the neuroscience discovery of empathic brain activity. There was no instrument that looked at the components as we describe them in chapter 1. Because we had become aware that these components operate in different ways and at varying levels, we thought we needed to be able to break them out in identifiable ways. For us as teachers, that made sense. We could focus on the development of specific components, which were more clearly defined, with a view toward the end result, which would be an overall change in empathy.

What brought us to a halt in that pursuit was the lack of any instruments that we could use to measure the discrete brain activities in a useable, self-report format. We could not use f MRIs and other brain imaging equipment in which we are not trained, are very expensive, and typically located in neurological laboratories or medical facilities. We discovered that we were not alone in that limitation. The result has been that self-report instruments are still the most common way to measure empathy in practice, but those instruments reflect definitions and conceptualizations of empathy that date back decades and do not reflect the cognitive neuroscience research of the past ten years. That is what drove us to develop an instrument that is based on the current neuroscience of empathy and can be used easily in the field.

This chapter starts with background on the measurement of empathy over the past several decades, which provides a foundation for our work.

We review the most commonly used instruments, and then move into our process of development and validation of three related instruments: the Empathy Assessment Index (EAI), the Social Empathy Index (SEI), and the Interpersonal and Social Empathy Index (ISEI). We provide an overview of each of the instruments, discuss how to use each one, and include ways to incorporate them into the teaching of empathy. First, however, we look at several other instruments.

EARLY EMPATHY-MEASURING INSTRUMENTS

For decades, researchers have relied on two major methods to determine if people possess empathic abilities. One was self-report, and the other was observation of people's reactions to prescribed situations. In order to identify empathy in children, early research relied on children's descriptions of their feelings after viewing pictures or hearing stories designed to elicit certain emotions (for example, the Feshbach Affective Situations Test of Empathy; Feshbach & Roe, 1968). Over the years, this procedure was criticized as being too narrow and subjective (the recorder decided if the child's response fit the empathic profile), as well as risking the child responding with perceived acceptable responses to the researcher. Other methods have been developed to address these limitations. Eisenberg and her colleagues (Eisenberg, Fabes, Bustamante, Mathy, Miller, & Lindholm, 1988; Eisenberg, Fabes, Schaller, Miller, & Carlo, 1991) have videotaped sequences reviewing children's somatic responses and have used sophisticated coding with multiple reviewers to analyze children's spontaneous responses to viewing the distress of others. More recently, they used the assessment of facial reactions coupled with self-report by the children of their feelings while watching slides of emotion-evoking actions (Zhou et al. 2002). The authors themselves acknowledge the limitation that the children's empathic responses may have been con-founded by their abilities to express themselves, with those able to better express what they are feeling being considered to be more empathic, although that may not have been the case. In general, validity may be compromised as children age and are better at controlling their expressions of emotion (Eisenberg, 1986). Thus, although observations of reactions in children can be helpful in identifying empathy, there are limitations.

Early research observing the empathic behaviors of adults also had significant limitations. The biggest problem was due to differences in conceptualizing empathy. Researchers were measuring different aspects of empathy, such as affective arousal or emotion sharing, but considering all the outcomes in terms of a single notion of empathy. The three most widely used instruments used to measure empathy are: (1) the Hogan Empathy Scale (HES; Hogan, 1969); (2) the Questionnaire Measure of Emotional Empathy (QMEE; Mehrabian & Epstein, 1972); and (3) the Interpersonal Reactivity Index (IRI; Davis, 1980, 1983). All three of these measures utilize self-report, a Likert-type scale, and have demonstrated varied levels of validity and reliability.

Early assessments of the use of the HES and QMEE found the instruments to be valid, but not comparable (Chlopan, McCain, Carbonell, & Hagen, 1985) in that each measured different aspects of empathy. The HES seemed to measure perspective-taking and the QMEE accounted for emotional arousal to others' distress. The low correlation between the results of tests using two instruments supports the fact that they measure different aspects of empathy. Additional research considered the HES to be a means for measuring cognitive empathy because it focuses on one person's intellectual or imaginative concern for another person's condition (Cliffordson, 2001; Davis, 1983). Moreoever, there was growing recognition that empathy is multifaceted and may require measurements that accommodate multiple related constructs (Deutsch & Madle, 1975).

In 2004, Jollife and Farrington completed a meta-analysis of thirty-five studies on empathy and criminal offending and concluded that the HES does not even measure empathy (or the lack of it) in criminal offender populations and therefore should not be used. In the same study, Jollife and Farrington argued that the QMEE measures at times appear to equate empathy with sympathy.

The Interpersonal Reactivity Index (IRI)

The most frequently used measure is the self-report Interpersonal Reactivity Instrument (IRI; Davis, 1980, 1983). The IRI consists of four subscales, each with seven items, making the instrument a total of twenty-eight items. The four subscales with an example of each are:

1 Perspective-taking (PT): "I believe that there are two sides to every question and try to look at them both."

2 Fantasy (F): "I really get involved with the feelings of the characters in a novel."

3 Empathic concern (EC): "I often have tender, concerned feelings for people less fortunate than me."

4 Personal distress (PD): "In emergency situations, I feel apprehensive and ill-at-ease."

Davis's rationale behind the IRI is that there are two aspects of empathy, affective and cognitive. The affective involves reactions motivated by seeing personal distress, and the cognitive is an intellectual process of perspective-taking or role-playing. His scale is thus multifaceted in attempting to bring both of these perspectives of empathy together. The first two subscales, PT and F, are designed to measure the cognitive aspects of empathy, and the third and fourth subscales are designed to measure the affective aspects of empathy. However, what we know today about mirror neurons suggests that a reexamination of this scale is warranted. If in healthy development we are all hard-wired to mirror, then the subscale of fantasy, putting one-self in the position of another, is a given—although awareness of that may not be. The awareness of that ability comes into play through cognitive processing, which includes perspective-taking but in theory also elements of the empathic concern subscale. However, several of the items in the EC scale address sympathy and pity rather than empathy ("I have tender, concerned feelings for people less fortunate than me"; "I would describe myself as a pretty soft-hearted person"; and the reverse-scored item, "When I see someone being treated unfairly, I sometimes don't feel very much pity for them").

Neuroscience suggests that the IRI subscales of fantasy and empathic concern are more affective, although self-recognition of the ability to mirror starts to move into the cognitive realm. Thus, while the first three subscales of the IRI are related to our current definition of empathy, they are conceptualized differently. The last subscale of personal distress (PD) reflects the literature on motivation for empathic behaviors and altruism. The rationale behind this is that when we see a person in distress, we are driven to alleviate both the discomfort we are feeling and the person's discomfort, so we are motivated to help others (Batson, 1991; Eisenberg & Fabes, 1998; Murphy, Shapard, Eisenberg, Fabes, & Guthrie, 1999). But we know that taking action to alleviate one's own distress may be completely self-focused even if instigated by observing the plight of another person.

Because of shifts in conceptualizing empathy as the sharing of emotions and stepping into the role of another, many researchers use only the two subscales of PT and EC, making their empathy measurement fourteen items (see for example, Jolliffe & Farrington, 2006; Laible, Carlo, & Roesch, 2004; Mayberry & Espelage, 2007), while some use only one subscale, such as the EC (Einolf, 2008; Righetti, Hofmann, Gere, Visserman, & Van Lange, 2016). Thus, the use of the IRI is often partial and more focused on perspective-taking and compassion or sympathy. Although these items do reflect aspects of empathy, they are not clearly aligned with what we now know from cognitive neuroscience.

Other Measures of Empathy

Given the criticism of the most widely used measures of empathy in the helping professional literature, others have developed empathy instruments. Thus, for example, Jollife and Farrington (2006) developed and validated a new measure of empathy for adolescents, the Basic Empathy Scale (BES). The BES is a self-report, Likert-type scale with twenty items. There is little evidence that the scale is being widely used. Other efforts include the Toronto Empathy Questionnaire (Spreng, McKinnon, Mar, & Levine, 2009), which is in part a variation on existing instruments and uses items from the QMEE and the IRI. Another instrument, the Empathy Quotient (EQ), is designed for clinical application, with particular emphasis on identifying a lack of empathy as an indicator of psychopathology, and therefore includes numerous items related to interpersonal behaviors (such as "I find it hard to know what to do in a social situation"; "When I was a child, I enjoyed cutting up worms to see what would happen"; and "If I say something that someone else is offended by, I think that that's their problem, not mine") (Baron-Cohen, 2011).

Recently, the Questionnaire of Cognitive and Affective Empathy (QCAE) was developed to measure cognitive and affective empathy and thus to encompass all the aspects of empathy (Reniers, Corcoran, Drake, Shryane, & Völlm, 2011). The researchers used items from the existing instruments, the HES, EQ, and IRI. In the end, we regard this as a rearrangement of the existing measures, but with a clearer acknowledgment of the different affective and cognitive processes of empathy. However, we think the items would benefit from an update in light of the findings from cognitive neuroscience. In particular, none of the instruments identifies emotion regulation as a distinct component of empathy, although neurological evidence shows that it is.

HOW CAN WE MEASURE EMPATHY IN LIGHT OF COGNITIVE NEUROSCIENCE FINDINGS?

The instruments we reviewed rely on definitions of empathy that are over a decade old—sometimes two or three decades—and focus on measuring specific aspects of empathy, such as affective response, cognitive processes, and, most often, perspective-taking alone. And sympathy, pity, and compassion are often used interchangeably with empathy, in spite of the differences. Although there are two main components of empathy—an emotional process of feeling another's emotions and responding with a congruent emotion; and the cognitive ability to take the perspective or point of view of another person ("putting yourself in someone else's shoes")—rarely do existing instruments clearly identify and include them both. Rather, they are split between focusing on affective response or on perspective-taking, but neither fully combines the two. Nor do they address the role of emotion regulation or advance the need for self-other awareness. And there is no instrument that looks at context and social structures to assess social empathy. Because today's research includes all those components of empathy, we set out to develop instruments that could be used to measure the full scope of interpersonal empathy and social empathy.

The Empathy Assessment Index (EAI): An Overview

The Empathy Assessment Index (EAI) was developed to update current measures of empathy to reflect recent neuroscience research, which documents that observable brain activity can be linked to specified components of empathy (Decety & Jackson, 2004). Our initial work was based on four components of empathy that had been identified in the cognitive neuroscience literature: (1) affective response, i.e., automatic reactions based on one's observation of another; (2) self-other awareness, or the ability to differentiate the experiences of another from one's own; (3) perspective-taking, the cognitive process of imagining the experiences of another; and

(4) emotion regulation, the ability to sense another's feelings without becoming overwhelmed by the intensity of this experience (Decety & Moriguchi, 2007). Our rationale for using these four components was to increase clarity in conceptualizing interpersonal empathy (Gerdes, Segal, & Lietz, 2010).

The EAI is based on Gerdes & Segal's (2009, 2011) model, which incorporates emotional and cognitive components of empathy. The EAI was developed through a series of applications conducted to improve upon the psychometric properties of the EAI measure. In 2009, the first round used an exploratory factor analysis (EFA) on a fifty-four-item preliminary version of the EAI (Gerdes, Lietz, & Segal, 2011). Although this initial version demonstrated some promise, the EFA identified some limitations of the initial measure, and several items needed to be changed or eliminated. In this original EFA study, the researchers included items from the Empathic Concern and Perspective-Taking components of the Interpersonal Reactivity Index (Davis, 1980, 1983). The items were used to demonstrate concurrent validity for the EAI's affective response (AR) and perspective-taking (PT) components. The results indicated statistically significant correlations between the Interpersonal Reactivity Index components of empathic concern and perspective-taking and the AR and PT components of the EAI. The other components of the IRI did not complement the cognitive neuroscience components of self-other awareness and emotion regulation. Other standardized tests were used to validate those components, including the Cognitive Emotion Regulation Questionnaire (CERQ; Garnefski & Kraaji, 2006), along with items from the Mindfulness Attention and Awareness Scale (MAAS; Brown & Ryan, 2003).

The objective of the next study was to build upon the previous research by eliminating items that did not contribute significantly to the measure and improving those that remained (Lietz, Gerdes, Sun, Geiger, Wagaman, & Segal, 2011). This round of development and testing of the EAI enhanced the reliability and validity of measuring empathy based on the four-part cognitive neuroscience definition of empathy. The result was a self-report Likert-Scale instrument with twenty items representing the four components of affective response, self-other awareness, perspective-taking, and emotion regulation.

Focus groups of service providers, students in research courses, and students at community GED classes reviewed the instrument with attention to language and ease of understanding. These efforts helped to develop wording that was clear and understandable to all levels of the groups involved in testing the EAI.

The final stage of validation involved administering the EAI to groups thought to have lower levels of empathy (samples of participants involved in court-mandated treatment programs for domestic violence or sex offenses) to see if there were statistical differences between their empathy scores and samples of professional social service providers. This known-group analysis was conducted to assess criterion validity. Based on a large body of research, we assumed that people involved in committing acts of domestic violence or sexual predation would have lower levels of empathy compared to professional social service providers. Analysis revealed that indeed the professionals scored statistically significantly higher than participants in the known groups, confirming the criterion validity of the EAI (Gerdes, Geiger, Lietz, Wagaman, & Segal, 2012).

The findings from another round of data collection were used to assess how to better address the multiple components of empathy in terms of newly emerging neuroscience research (Walter, 2012; Decety, 2011). From this work, we further developed the EAI to ensure that some of the affective response items more accurately reflect the physiological reaction to an actual perceived event, separate from having a physiological reaction after hearing or reading about a description of an event and consequently developing a mental image of that event. The state of imagining or thinking about an experience is actually "affective mentalizing" and is also neurologically observable (Schnell, Bluschke, Konradt, & Walter, 2011).

Affective mentalizing is the process of cognitively appraising someone's emotional state (Frith & Frith, 2006). We infer others' emotional states through nonverbal cues (facial expressions, for example) as well as knowledge about other people's situation and beliefs. When experiencing affective mentalizing, one may even have physiological reactions that mirror the imagined affect. Mentalizing can take place without much direct stimulus. For example, reading about a person's situation, or listening to someone talk about it on the phone, or hearing someone else describing a person's situation can all evoke mental pictures of affective experiences. Therefore, to capture this aspect of empathy, we added a new component of affective mentalizing. In the fall of 2012 we administered the five-component version of the EAI, and found it to be reliable and valid with a sample of 450 college students. This round finalized the development of the EAI to include five components with a total of twenty-two items: (1) affective response, (2) affective mentalizing, (3) self-other awareness, (4) perspective-taking, and (5) emotion regulation.

Overall, the development and testing of the EAI spanned a four-year period with eight different administrations to more than 3,500 participants. Ongoing research includes using the EAI as a measure to compare before and after interventions designed to enhance empathy.

The Social Empathy Index (SEI): An Overview

The Social Empathy Index (SEI) was developed to assess levels of empathy on a macro level. As we know, social empathy is the ability to understand people from different socioeconomic classes, racial/ethnic backgrounds, and other diversities and to have insight into the context of institutionalized inequalities and disparities (Segal, 2007, 2011). Because interpersonal empathy can be limited when the context of experiences is not also assessed (Singer & Lamm, 2009), and a lack of understanding cultural differences, social situations, and political and economic conditions can hamper the accuracy of people's empathic insights (Hollan, 2012), we wanted to expand our measurement to include social empathy. The skills it involves are similar to those of interpersonal empathy: the ability to take the perspective of those who differ from us in life experiences while maintaining an awareness of the differences between oneself and others. Contextual understanding and macro perspective-taking can build upon interpersonal empathy skills to develop social empathy. We believe that increasing social empathy can lead to positive societal change and promote social well-being. The value of teaching social empathy and creating interventions that promote social empathy is enhanced by the ability to measure and assess it—hence the development of the SEI.

The SEI includes the twenty-two items from the Empathy Assessment Index that measure interpersonal empathy, in addition to the two macro components of contextual understanding of systemic barriers and macro self-other awareness/perspective-taking (Segal, Wagaman, & Gerdes, 2012).

In January of 2012, another round of measurement was conducted to test the finalized version of the SEI (which included the EAI). An exploratory factor analysis was conducted to confirm the selection of items (Segal, Wagaman, & Gerdes, 2012). Initially, thirty-eight items designed to measure social empathy were included in this round of testing. Through statistical analysis and expert review, the pool of social empathy items were reduced to eighteen items divided between the contextual understanding and macro self-other awareness/perspective-taking components. The final result was a forty-item self-report Likert-scale instrument combining the five components of the EAI and the two components of social empathy.

Administration of the EAI and the SEI

The EAI and the SEI can be administered in a simple paper and pencil version or on-line through a survey instrument software program. The researchers have used both methods without any problems arising. In order to diminish social desirability, that is the tendency for people to answer what they think you want to hear rather than what they are really feeling, the instrument has been titled a "Human Relations Survey." This provides a nondescript title so that participants are not aware of the link to empathy, thereby controlling for any biases or preconceived notions about what empathy is and is not. Also, when administering the EAI and the SEI, all references to the components are dropped. We include those component references in brackets on the copies of the EAI and the SEI in this book so you can see the operationalization of the separate components.

The first part (items 1–22) concerns interpersonal empathy and has five components: affective response (AR), affective mentalizing (AM), self-other awareness (SOA), perspective-taking (PT), and emotion regulation (ER). Two items under the ER component are to be reverse-scored. The second part (items 23–40) contains two components: contextual understanding of systemic barriers (CU) and macro self-other awareness/perspective-taking (MSP).

The Likert scale used ranges from 1 (never) to 6 (always) with choices 2–5 in between. The wording for the Likert scale and the use of 6 choices were established through focus groups, and this format has been used as part of the reliability and validation testing. Therefore, we suggest that the SEI should be used in its entirety as created by the authors.

What Do the Components Mean?

In chapter 1 we identified and explained the components that make up inter-personal and social empathy. What follows is a review of each component.

1   *Affective response.* The brain includes neurological pathways that are capable of physiologically simulating the experiences of others. Often referred to as "mirroring" in the literature, this ability is unconscious, automatic, and involuntary. For example, if a person starts crying in front of you, even if you do not understand why, you too will feel like crying. Affective sharing can run through all types of emotions (happy, sad) as well as physical sensations (feeling pain when watching another person being physically hurt). Humans appear to be hard-wired to mimic one another, which in turn sets the stage for experientially connecting to another person.

2   *Affective mentalizing.* Not all physiological reactions or mirroring come from the actual viewing of an event or experience. Often we are exposed to stories or explanations of events, and as we are hearing the information, our mind develops a picture of them, which allows us to develop perceptions of another's experiences and may also trigger an affective or physiological response. When this occurs, we are mentalizing, or imagining the event and potentially experiencing it as if it is happening to us as well.

3   *Self-other awareness.* Once the affective response occurs, we need to recognize the difference between the experiences of another person and our own. We may feel like crying (as in the example above), but the experience that prompted the other person to have an emotion is the other person's experience and not our own. This moves empathic response into a cognitive or conscious arena.

4   *Perspective-taking.* Assuming that one successfully mirrors and then processes the affective response to understand that it belongs to the other person, it becomes possible to cognitively process what it might be like to personally experience the experiences of another. This is what we commonly refer to as "stepping into the shoes of another."

5   *Emotion regulation.* The last component of interpersonal empathy helps us to move through these affective and cognitive processes and sense another's feelings without becoming overwhelmed or swept up into that person's emotions.

6 *Contextual understanding of systemic barriers.* To fully grasp the life experiences of groups different from ourselves, we need to understand the impact of social, political, and economic barriers and privileges on them historically and now.

7 *Macro self-other awareness/perspective-taking.* By gaining insight into the social, political and economic context we can step more fully into the experiences of others who are different from us and cognitively process what it might be like to live as a member of another group.

Although additional research is needed to understand how much of each component is necessary for the full effect of social empathy, by isolating the five components of the EAI with the two additional components of the SEI, we can determine which areas might need more attention and improvement. This knowledge can be used to inform training and interventions, which can help to raise overall levels of interpersonal empathy and social empathy.

What Do the Scores Mean?

Studies to develop an understanding of what different scores may mean have yet to be conducted. Although this may be possible after numerous applications in a variety of settings and with different populations, we are wary of developing norms or cutting scores. Interpersonal and social empathy as parts of human behavior are contextual, and therefore standardized scoring would not be appropriate. We feel the EAI and SEI are best used as overall gauges that can help identify the stronger and weaker aspects of an individual's empathic abilities. By distinguishing each component, it is possible to focus on the components that most need development in order to cultivate the full scope of empathy. For example, while two people might have the same total score, one might have very high scores in affective response, but not so high in emotion regulation, while the other has the opposite. Providing training to enhance mindfulness of affective reactions would help only one of the two, as would training to help with emotion regulation. Isolating the components with subscales can help focus training and minimize the risk of training for the wrong skill.

The EAI and SEI are also useful for measuring changes that might occur following interventions designed to enhance interpersonal and social empathy. We encourage the use of the EAI and SEI with multiple populations in diverse settings to gain better insight into the utility and efficacy of the instruments.

The Interpersonal and Social Empathy Index (ISEI)

While working with community groups interested in using the instruments, we found an interest in assessing both interpersonal and social empathy, but a limitation in using an instrument that included forty items. Many social service providers have multiple measures that they must administer to clients as part of funding requirements, so adding an additional instrument presents time and client-attention challenges. To address these, we worked on adapting the longer version to a sound and helpful shorter instrument. The Interpersonal and Social Empathy Index (ISEI) provides a measure that assesses elements of interpersonal and social empathy from the EAI and the SEI.

The ISEI was validated on data gathered from a sample of 450 undergraduate students in the fall of 2012. Exploratory and confirmatory factor analyses were performed on components of interpersonal and social empathy in order to validate their interconnectedness. The result was identification of fifteen items that best measured interpersonal and social empathy (Segal, Cimino, Gerdes, Harmon, & Wagaman, 2013). These fifteen items make up the ISEI and are divided among four components: macro perspective-taking, self-other awareness, affective response, and cognitive empathy. The first three are defined above. *Cognitive empathy* occurs when we process affective input on a conscious level to try to understand what another person's mental and emotional state. Doing so requires skills in perspective-taking, self-other awareness, and emotion regulation.

We recommend using the EAI for a full assessment of interpersonal empathy, and the SEI for a full assessment of social empathy. The ISEI, which is shorter, provides a more general view of the two kinds of empathy and is useful in situations where time is a major consideration. In the following appendices are all three instruments with the components identified. We have also indicated with an R those items that should be reverse-scored. Remember to de-identify those items when using the instruments and to refrain from using the word *empathy* in naming the instruments to prevent bias in participants. A Spanish translation of the EAI and SEI appears in the last appendix. The fifteen items for the ISEI can be pulled from the translation as well.

FURTHER EXPLORATION

The academic world is now more attuned to examining research findings across disciplines. Integrating cognitive neuroscience's findings on empathy with what we know about human behavior in the social environment has helped us to expand our analysis and view empathy as consisting of interpersonal and social empathy, with each of these being made up of identifiable components. However, we are likely in the earliest stages of understanding empathy from a neurological perspective. That means that with advances in technology for reading brain activity, we may come to different interpretations and conclusions in the future.

While cognitive neuroscience has enriched what we know today about empathy and human beings in the social context, the extent to which environment and social conditions play a role in the development and expression of empathy still need greater investigation. Moreover, there is still more to be understood about the inherent biological aspects of empathy. If we can better identify the roles of biology and social context, we can better identify ways to teach empathy. Thus, we are excited about future possibilities for expanding the development and application of interventions that can enhance peoples' abilities to experience the full scope of empathy.

CONCLUDING REMARKS

At this point, we feel confident that you have the background and understanding to be an active participant in assessing and measuring empathy. We believe that the tools of the EAI, SEI and ISEI provide an excellent starting place to identify, assess, and measure all the aspects of empathy that have been identified up to this point in time. We look forward to seeing the results of studies using these instruments, as replication and wide application are the best ways to further our collective knowledge. And we hope the information and instruments in this book, along with the knowledge that empathy can be taught and learned, make you better prepared to engage in the process of helping to build stronger empathic abilities and networks.

Research and Statistical Analysis of the Relationship Between Interpersonal Empathy and Social Empathy

METHODS

Data Collection

In the fall of 2012, data were collected in an institutional review board–approved study at a large public university. Using a Qualtrics-based online survey approach, 725 undergraduate students in seven undergraduate classes were invited to participate. Participants were not required to take the survey, although all of the instructors offered extra credit for participation. Four hundred and sixty four students completed the survey (64 percent response rate).

Fourteen students had multiple missing responses and were excluded from the analysis (3.1 percent). There was a small amount of missing data in the remaining 450 cases, and this was handled using multiple imputation. Specifically, ten imputed datasets were created with missing observations filled in on the basis of statistically plausible values from the appropriate posterior multivariate normal distribution. Analyses were then run separately on each of the ten datasets and combined using standard procedures.

Participants

The 450 participants ranged in age from 18 to 61 years ($M=23$, $SD=5.69$). Sixty-six percent ($n=296$) of the sample were female, 33.8 percent ($n=152$) were male and .2 percent ($n=1$) reported other gender. Of those who reported

TABLE APP.1 INTERPERSONAL AND SOCIAL EMPATHY ITEMS
                 FOLLOWING EXPLORATORY FACTOR ANALYSIS

When I see someone receive a gift that makes them happy, I feel happy myself.

When I am with someone who gets sad news, I feel sad for a moment too.

Hearing laughter makes me smile.

I can consider my point of view and another person's point of view at the same time.

When I see a person experiencing a strong emotion, I can accurately assess what that person is feeling.

I can tell the difference between someone else's feelings and my own.

I am aware of what other people think of me.

I am aware of other people's emotions.

I can explain to others how I am feeling.

I take action to help others even if it does not personally benefit me.

I am comfortable helping a person of a different race or ethnicity than my own.

I feel it is important to understand the political perspectives of people I don't agree with.

I believe that people who face discrimination have added stress that negatively impacts their lives.

I believe government should protect the rights of minorities.

their ethnicity, 52.4 percent identified as Caucasian ($n=236$), 16.2 percent as Latino ($n=73$), 8 percent as Asian ($n=36$), 7.8 percent as Middle Eastern ($n=35$), 7.6 percent as multiracial ($n=34$), 5.3 percent as African American ($n=24$), 1.6 percent as American Indian ($n=7$), and .4 percent as "other" ($n=2$). Of the 450 cases, .7 percent chose not to answer the question on race and ethnicity ($n=3$). Just over 24 percent were freshmen ($n=109$), 27 percent were sophomores ($n=121$), 28 percent were juniors ($n=126$), and 20 percent were seniors ($n=91$). Participants identified more than 40 different academic areas of primary study. The five largest groups were: 18.9 percent ($n=121$) reported criminal justice as their academic major; 15.3 percent ($n=69$) reported social work; 9.7 percent ($n=43$) reported engineering; 8.9 percent ($n=40$) reported psychology; and 5.3 percent ($n=24$) reported business.

Twenty-eight percent of the sample (n=125) reported their family of origin's socioeconomic status (SES) as poor (8 percent) or working class (20 percent). Forty-two percent of the participants (n=118) reported their family of origin SES as middle class, and 26 percent (n=117) reported as upper class. Four percent of the sample did not respond to the SES item.

Measures

Data were collected on 32 combined items from the Empathy Assessment Index (EAI) and the Social Empathy Index (SEI). The combined items were reduced based on the findings of an exploratory factor analysis (see table App. 1). The reduction of items allowed for a more efficient statistical analysis. The items used in the current study were selected based on the findings of an exploratory factor analysis completed on all thirty-two items. The results identified four factors (eigenvalues: AR=1.19; COG=1.99, SOA=1.93, MPT=5.50) and explained 43.26 percent of the variance. The alpha reliability estimates for the four factors were as follows: AR α=.64; COG α=.76; SOA α=.69; MPT α=.77.

Data Analysis Plan

Mplus version 7.0 was used to complete the analysis. The researchers' first theoretical interest was in optimally classifying the sample into three latent classes for interpersonal empathy (IE) and for social empathy (SE), respectively. The three categories separate individuals who tend to self-report low, medium, or high scores on the observed variables that correspond to interpersonal empathy and to social empathy. Latent class analysis, which is similar to factor analysis when the underlying unobserved variables are categorical, was used to optimally classify the sample into the appropriate categories. Beyond classification of interpersonal and social empathy, race, gender, and one's family of origin socioeconomic status were expected to affect whether an individual self-reported low, medium, or high scores on the empathy items.

These expectations called for a full structural equation model in which the latent classes are defined on the basis of multiple observed variables and simultaneously serve as the dependent variables in a regression on the demographics. However, there is some methodological controversy over whether the measurement model should be estimated separately from the multinomial logistic regression (Asparouhov & Muthen, 2012; Vermunt, 2010). The issue revolves around the fact that the distribution of classes is often of fundamental interest in addition to the full structural model, yet the optimal structural model may lead to classifications that are different depending on which independent variables are included. Thus, Vermunt (2010) argues in favor of a three-step approach in which the measurement model is estimated first, followed by classifying observations on the basis of their most likely class membership, and finally regressing these classes on the independent variables using a weight matrix determined by the classification uncertainty found in step two.

While ideal for this study, the three-step approach has been fully developed only in the context of a single latent class variable. Thus, the researchers estimated the full structural equation model in a single step. Nonetheless, the results of the measurement model estimated alone were compared to the results of the measurement model estimated within the larger structural model, and the distribution of scores was found to be very similar and the relationship between interpersonal empathy and social empathy held. The stability of the classifications is due to the fact that the measurement model separated the observations quite well, producing high levels of relative entropy (see tables in the Results section below) that imply low classification error. Vermunt's (2010) simulation study showed that the three-step approach converges to the more efficient one-step approach as class separation improves.

Finally, for both the interpersonal and social empathy items, the observed variables were measured using a Likert scale: 1 = never; 2 = rarely; 3 = sometimes; 4 = frequently; 5 = almost always; to 6 = always. Within the sample, however, there were very few responses in the lowest two categories (never, rarely) of the observed variables. This caused problems during estimation of the measurement model, as there was too little information to locate the threshold parameters in the ordered logit models. Thus, categories 1, 2, and 3 (never, rarely, sometimes) were combined and into a single category and recoded as 1. The newly recoded Likert scale had four values: 1 = never, rarely, sometimes; 2 = frequently; 3 = almost always; 4 = always.

Determining the Number of Classes

Although the hypothesis was that the observations would separate cleanly into three categories, it was also plausible that a simpler, two-class model would yield a satisfactory fit. To test for this possibility, three-class measurement models were estimated first to be compared to subsequently estimated two-class models. The predicted probabilities of each resulting class choosing a specific ordinal category on the observed variables were used to label the classes. Figure App.1 shows these probabilities for the interpersonal variables, and figure App.2 shows them for social empathy. The X-axis in figure App.1 represents the nine items used to measure interpersonal empathy. The Y-axis represents the predicted probabilities of each resulting class choosing the identified ordinal category: $Pr(Y=4)$, or always; $Pr(Y=3)$,

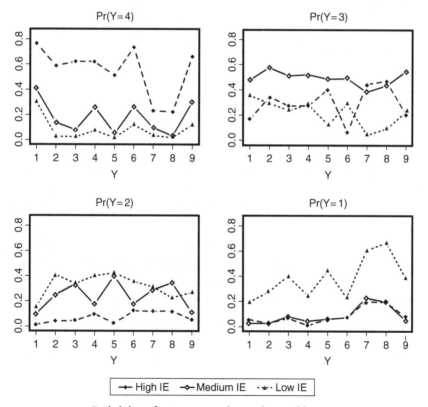

FIGURE APP.1 Probabilities for interpersonal empathy variables

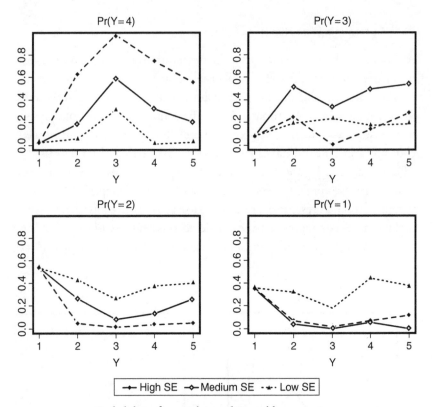

FIGURE APP.2 Probabilities for social empathy variables

or almost always; Pr(Y=2), or frequently; Pr(Y=1), or never, rarely, and sometimes. Likewise, in figure App.2 the X-axis represents the five items used to measure social empathy and the Y-axis represents predicted probabilities.

As figure App.1 demonstrates, the class coded as "high interpersonal empathy" had the highest probability of choosing 4 (always) across all nine of the indicator variables. This same group generally had the lowest probability of choosing 1 (never, rarely, sometimes). Likewise, the class coded as "low interpersonal empathy" had the highest probability of choosing 1 and the lowest probability of choosing 4 across the variables. The "medium interpersonal empathy" group was somewhere in between for the probabilities of choosing a 1 or 4; their usual choice was 3 for most variables. The class labels thus seem appropriate on the basis of these probabilities. Figure

App.2, which shows the predicted probabilities for the social empathy indicators by latent class, is interpreted in a similar fashion.

Comparing Two- and Three-Class Models

After verifying that the three classes do indeed demonstrate stable patterns in predicting categories on the observed variables, a simpler two-class model was run for comparison. Table App.2 displays the sample distribution across classes in both the two- and three-class models along with relative entropy and Bayesian Information Criteria. The former is a measure of the strength of class separation that ranges from zero to one, with a one representing perfect (i.e., error-free) separation. The latter is presented in smaller-is-better form.

In the two-class model, 42.2 percent of observations received a classification of "low interpersonal empathy," compared to 57.8 percent in the "high interpersonal" category. Separating observations into three interpersonal empathy categories yields 35 percent of the sample in the low category, 47.2 percent in the medium category, and 17.8 percent in the high category. The Bayesian Information Criterion (BIC) shows a clear preference for the three-class model, falling from 11183.937 in the two-class case to 11070.079 for three classes. In addition, entropy improves from .826 to .839. Thus, the data presented in table App.2 clearly favor a three-class measurement model.

TABLE APP.2   Distribution of Sample Across Latent Classes:
Two and Three-Class Models

	EAI		SE	
	2 CLASS	3 CLASS	2 CLASS	3 CLASS
Low	42.2%	35.0%	42.3%	25.9%
Medium		47.2%		29.9%
High	57.8%	17.8%	57.7%	44.1%
Entropy	0.826	0.839	0.750	0.737
BIC	11183.937	11071.079	5599.741	5574.805

Looking at the social empathy columns, 42.3 percent were classified as having low social empathy, while 57.7 percent were classified as having high social empathy. The distribution for the three-class model yielded a little over 25 percent of observations in the low category, 29.9 percent in the medium category, and 44.1 percent in the high category. The BIC again supports the three-class model (5574.805 for three classes versus 5599.741 for two). Entropy, however, does decline a little in the case of three classes, meaning that the separation is less clear. Nonetheless, this reduction is small and, with the obvious BIC improvement, three classes are retained.

Table App.3 displays results for the multinomial logit model of interpersonal empathy. The first thing to notice is the clear, statistically significant effect of SE in predicting IE. Those who fall into the high SE category are much more likely to fall into the high IE category over the low IE category (B = 4.576, SE = .930, p < .001). The odds ratio of 97.125 shows that high SE subjects are vastly more likely to be high IE compared to low SE. Those with medium SE are also significantly more likely to be high IE compared

TABLE APP.3   Multinomial Logit Model of SE

	PARAMETER	SE	ODDS RATIO	T SCORE	PROBABILITY
Latino	1.55*	0.584	4.711	2.654	0.008
Asian	0.679	0.690	1.972	0.984	0.325
Middle Eastern	0.349	0.508	1.418	0.687	0.492
Other	0.854	0.496	2.349	1.720	0.085
SES	−0.197	0.221	0.821	−0.889	0.374
SEX	0.428	0.339	1.534	1.261	0.207
Intercept	0.232	0.706	1.261	0.328	0.743
MEDIUM VS. LOW					
Latino	1.525*	0.569	4.595	2.681	0.007
Asian	1.300	0.705	3.669	1.843	0.065
Middle Eastern	0.053	0.762	1.054	0.070	0.944
Other	−0.532	0.643	0.587	−0.827	0.408
SES	−0.246	0.248	0.782	−0.993	0.321
SEX	0.615	0.377	1.850	1.633	0.102
Intercept	0.520	0.629	1.682	0.827	0.408

* p < .05

Note: Low is reference category for dependent variable; white is reference category for ethnicity; and male is reference category for gender.

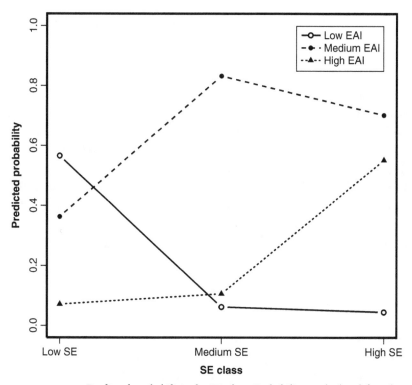

FIGURE APP.3 Predicted probabilities by SE class. Probabilities calculated for white female with median SES.

to low SE (B=2.559, SE=1.235, p=.035). The odds ratio is again very large (OR=13.45), though much smaller relative to the odds ratio for high SE.

A similar pattern occurs for the model that compares medium IE to low IE. High SE subjects are significantly more likely to be medium IE (B=2.630, SE=.753, p<.001), as are medium SE subjects (B=3.034, SE=.764, p<.001). The odds ratios show that the odds of a high SE subject being medium IE are again substantially higher compared to low SE (OR=13.784). The odds of a medium subject being medium IE are even larger (OR=20.780).

Because the coefficients and odds ratios depend on the IE category chosen as the reference, figure App.3 displays the predicted probabilities for each IE class by SE classes. Predicted probabilities in logit models depend not only on the independent variable of interest, but also on the values of the other independent variables in the model. Thus, these probabilities were calculated for a white female whose SES is equal to the median.

The predicted probability that somebody with low SE also has low IE is .566. This probability drops to .363 when considering the probability that somebody with low SE has medium IE. It drops further to .071 when considering the probability that a low SE subject has high IE. The predicted probability that somebody with medium SE has low IE is .062. The most likely category for a medium SE subject is medium IE (probability=.832). The probability falls to .106 for a medium SE having high IE. Finally, somebody with high SE has a predicted probability of .045 of having low IE. The probability increases to .402 for medium IE. The most likely IE class for somebody with high SE is high, where the probability is .552. Across the board, the most likely IE class corresponds exactly to the SE class.

The Structural Model Includes Ethnicity, Gender, and SES

The full structural model includes ethnicity, gender, and SES as predictors of each latent variable. In addition, the model allows IE categories to depend on SE categories. Because each of the two latent variables consists of three categories, the structural model is equivalent to a multinomial logit model. The results for the multinomial logit model of SE are displayed in table App.4. The baseline category used in the multinomial logit model was low SE, meaning that the coefficients and odds ratios should be interpreted with reference to this category.

The data in table App.4 show that only ethnicity appears to produce statistically significant changes in SE categories. Specifically, the coefficient on Latino is significant both for predicting high SE over low SE (B=1.55, SE=.584, p=.008) and for predicting medium SE over low SE (B=1.525, SE=.569, p=.007). Compared to whites, the odds of a Latino falling into the high SE category are substantially higher (OR=4.711). The odds ratio is also very high for the medium SE category (OR=4.595). The only other variable that approaches significance in either portion of the table is the Asian category in the medium SE model (B=1.3, SE=.705, p=.065). This coefficient estimate expects that the odds of an Asian falling into the medium rather than low category is 267 percent higher when compared to whites.

Ethnicity also appears to matter, especially when comparing medium IE to low IE. Latinos are significantly less likely to be medium IE relative to

TABLE APP.4   Multinomial Logit Model of IE

HIGH VS. LOW	PARAMETER	SE	ODDS RATIO	T	P
High SE	4.576***	0.930	97.125	4.920	0.000
Med. SE	2.599*	1.235	13.450	2.105	0.035
Latino	−0.895	0.768	0.409	−1.166	0.243
Asian	−1.436	1.133	0.238	−1.268	0.205
Mideast	−1.853	1.008	0.157	−1.838	0.066
Other	−1.074	0.852	0.342	−1.261	0.207
SES	−0.005	0.313	0.995	−0.015	0.988
Sex	1.243*	0.531	3.466	2.339	0.019
Intercept	−2.062	0.843	0.127	−2.445	0.014
MEDIUM VS. LOW					
High SE	2.630***	0.753	13.874	3.493	0.000
Med. SE	3.034***	0.764	20.780	3.970	0.000
Latino	−1.484*	0.601	0.227	−2.468	0.014
Asian	−2.064**	0.755	0.127	−2.734	0.006
Mideast	−2.278**	0.714	0.102	−3.192	0.001
Other	−1.182	0.785	0.307	−1.506	0.132
SES	−0.104	0.255	0.901	−0.409	0.683
Sex	0.329	0.422	1.390	0.778	0.437
Intercept	−0.236	0.644	0.790	−0.367	0.714

* p<.05

** p<.01

*** p<.001

Note: "Low" is reference category for dependent variable; "white" is reference category for ethnicity; and "male" is reference category for gender.

whites (B=−1.484, SE=.601, p=.014). Specifically, the odds of being medium IE are (1−.227=) 77.3 percent lower for Latinos relative to whites. The difference with whites is also significant for Asians (B=−2.064, SE=.755, p=.006) and for those from the Middle East (B=−2.278, SE=.755, p=.001). The odds of an Asian falling into the medium IE category are 87.3 percent lower compared to whites. The odds ratio is even lower (OR=.102) for those from the Middle East.

The only other variable to play a significant role is gender in the model for high IE. Females are more likely than men to exhibit high IE relative to low IE (B=1.243, SE=.531, =.019). Specifically, the odds are 246 percent higher for females relative to men.

TABLE APP.5   Distribution of Classes Under the Full
              Structural Equation Model

		INTERPERSONAL EMPATHY		
		LOW	MEDIUM	HIGH
Social	Low	22.2%	7.5%	1.3%
empathy	Medium	6.0%	24.8%	3.3%
	High	4.8%	12.9%	16.5%

After fitting the full structural model, one final test was carried out to determine if the full structural model had much of an impact on the distribution of class membership relative to estimation of the measurement model by itself. Table App.2 showed the distribution of classes when the measurement model was estimated without the demographic predictors. Table App.5 shows the class distribution in the full structural equation model. In comparing the two, it appears that there are some small differences in the cell values. Nonetheless, because the classes separate quite cleanly, the deviations are small and the general patterns remain. The upshot is that using the one-step maximum likelihood approach to estimating the structural model has only a minimal impact on the distribution of classes, and hence on inferences drawn about the relationship between IE and SE.

Empathy Assessment Index

Please respond to the following questions by selecting the choice that most closely reflects your feelings or beliefs.

NEVER	RARELY	SOMETIMES	FREQUENTLY	ALMOST ALWAYS	ALWAYS
1	2	3	4	5	6

1. When I see someone receive a gift that makes them happy, I feel happy myself. [AR]   1 2 3 4 5 6

2. Emotional stability describes me well. [ER]   1 2 3 4 5 6

3. I am good at understanding other people's emotions. [AM]   1 2 3 4 5 6

4. I can consider my point of view and another person's point of view at the same time. [PT]   1 2 3 4 5 6

5. When I get angry, I need a lot of time to get over it. [ER] R   1 2 3 4 5 6

6. I can imagine what the character is feeling in a good movie. [PT]   1 2 3 4 5 6

7. When I see someone being publicly embarrassed I cringe a little. [AR]   1 2 3 4 5 6

8. I can tell the difference between someone else's feelings and my own. [SOA]   1 2 3 4 5 6

9. When I see a person experiencing a strong emotion I can accurately assess what that person is feeling. [AM]   1 2 3 4 5 6

10. Friends view me as a moody person. [ER] R   1 2 3 4 5 6

11. When I see someone accidently hit his or her thumb with a hammer, I feel a flash of pain myself. [AR]   1 2 3 4 5 6

12. When I see a person experiencing a strong emotion, I can   1 2 3 4 5 6
    describe what the person is feeling to someone else. [AM]

13. I can imagine what it's like to be in someone else's   1 2 3 4 5 6
    shoes. [PT]

14. I can tell the difference between my friend's feelings and   1 2 3 4 5 6
    my own. [SOA]

15. I consider other people's points of view in discussions. [PT] 1 2 3 4 5 6

16. When I am with someone who gets sad news, I feel sad for a   1 2 3 4 5 6
    moment too. [AR]

17. When I am upset or unhappy, I get over it quickly. [ER]   1 2 3 4 5 6

18. I can explain to others how I am feeling. [SOA]   1 2 3 4 5 6

19. I can agree to disagree with other people. [PT]   1 2 3 4 5 6

20. I am aware of what other people think of me. [SOA]   1 2 3 4 5 6

21. Hearing laughter makes me smile. [AR]   1 2 3 4 5 6

22. I am aware of other people's emotions. [AM]   1 2 3 4 5 6

Contains 5 components: affective response [AR], affective mentalizing [AM], self-other awareness [SOA], perspective-taking [PT], and emotion regulation [ER].

AR = 5 items, AM = 4 items, SOA = 4 items, PT = 5 items, and ER = 4 items

Reverse scoring indicated by R

Social Empathy Index

Please respond to the following questions by selecting the choice that most closely reflects your feelings or beliefs.

NEVER	RARELY	SOMETIMES	FREQUENTLY	ALMOST ALWAYS	ALWAYS
1	2	3	4	5	6

1. When I see someone receive a gift that makes them happy, I feel happy myself. [AR]   1 2 3 4 5 6

2. Emotional stability describes me well. [ER]   1 2 3 4 5 6

3. I am good at understanding other people's emotions. [AM]   1 2 3 4 5 6

4. I can consider my point of view and another person's point of view at the same time. [PT]   1 2 3 4 5 6

5. When I get angry, I need a lot of time to get over it. [ER] R   1 2 3 4 5 6

6. I can imagine what the character is feeling in a good movie. [PT]   1 2 3 4 5 6

7. When I see someone being publicly embarrassed I cringe a little. [AR]   1 2 3 4 5 6

8. I can tell the difference between someone else's feelings and my own. [SOA]   1 2 3 4 5 6

9. When I see a person experiencing a strong emotion I can accurately assess what that person is feeling. [AM]   1 2 3 4 5 6

10. Friends view me as a moody person. [ER] R   1 2 3 4 5 6

11. When I see someone accidently hit his or her thumb with a hammer, I feel a flash of pain myself. [AR]   1 2 3 4 5 6

12. When I see a person experiencing a strong emotion, I can   1 2 3 4 5 6
    describe what the person is feeling to someone else. [AM]

13. I can imagine what it's like to be in someone else's shoes. [PT]   1 2 3 4 5 6

14. I can tell the difference between my friend's feelings and my   1 2 3 4 5 6
    own. [SOA]

15. I consider other people's points of view in discussions. [PT]   1 2 3 4 5 6

16. When I am with someone who gets sad news, I feel sad for a   1 2 3 4 5 6
    moment too. [AR]

17. When I am upset or unhappy, I get over it quickly. [ER]   1 2 3 4 5 6

18. I can explain to others how I am feeling. [SOA]   1 2 3 4 5 6

19. I can agree to disagree with other people. [PT]   1 2 3 4 5 6

20. I am aware of what other people think of me. [SOA]   1 2 3 4 5 6

21. Hearing laughter makes me smile. [AR]   1 2 3 4 5 6

22. I am aware of other people's emotions. [AM]   1 2 3 4 5 6

23. I believe adults who are in poverty deserve social assistance.   1 2 3 4 5 6
    [CU]

24. I confront discrimination when I see it. [MSP]   1 2 3 4 5 6

25. I think the government needs to be a part of leveling the   1 2 3 4 5 6
    playing field for people from different racial groups. [CU]

26. I believe it is necessary to participate in community service.   1 2 3 4 5 6
    [MSP]

27. I believe that people who face discrimination have added   1 2 3 4 5 6
    stress that negatively impacts their lives. [CU]

28. I am comfortable helping a person of a different race or   1 2 3 4 5 6
    ethnicity than my own. [MSP]

29. I take action to help others even if it does not personally   1 2 3 4 5 6
    benefit me. [MSP]

30. I can best understand people who are different from me by   1 2 3 4 5 6
    learning from them directly. [MSP]

31. I believe government should protect the rights of minorities.   1 2 3 4 5 6
    [CU]

32. I believe that each of us should participate in political   1 2 3 4 5 6
    activities. [MSP]

33. I believe people born into poverty have more barriers to   1 2 3 4 5 6
    achieving economic well-being than people who were not
    born into poverty. [CU]

34. I feel it is important to understand the political perspectives   1 2 3 4 5 6
    of people I don't agree with. [MSP]

35. I think it is the right of all citizens to have their basic needs   1 2 3 4 5 6
    met. [CU]

36. I believe the role of government is to act as a referee, making   1 2 3 4 5 6
    decisions that promote the quality of life and well-being of
    the people. [CU]

37. I have an interest in understanding why people cannot meet   1 2 3 4 5 6
    their basic needs financially. [MSP]

38. I believe that by working together, people can change   1 2 3 4 5 6
    society to be more just and fair for everyone. [CU]

39. I believe my actions will affect future generations. [MSP]   1 2 3 4 5 6

40. I believe there are barriers in the United States' educational   1 2 3 4 5 6
    system that prevent some groups of people from having
    economic success. [CU]

For questions 1–22, the instrument contains 5 components: affective response [AR], affective mentalizing [AM], self-other awareness [SOA], perspective-taking [PT], and emotion regulation [ER].

AR = 5 items, AM = 4 items, SOA = 4 items, PT = 5 items, and ER = 4 items

For questions 23–40, the instrument contains 2 components: contextual understanding of systemic barriers [CU] and macro self-other awareness/ perspective taking [MSP].

CU = 9 items and MSP = 9 items

Reverse scoring indicated by R

Interpersonal and Social Empathy Index

Please respond to the following questions by selecting the choice that most closely reflects your feelings or beliefs.

NEVER	RARELY	SOMETIMES	FREQUENTLY	ALMOST ALWAYS	ALWAYS
1	2	3	4	5	6

1. When I see someone receive a gift that makes them happy, I feel happy myself. [AR] 1 2 3 4 5 6

2. I am good at understanding other people's emotions. [COG] 1 2 3 4 5 6

3. I can consider my point of view and another person's point of view at the same time. [COG] 1 2 3 4 5 6

4. I am aware of what other people think of me. [SOA] 1 2 3 4 5 6

5. I can tell the difference between someone else's feelings and my own. [COG] 1 2 3 4 5 6

6. When I am with someone who gets sad news, I feel sad for a moment too. [AR] 1 2 3 4 5 6

7. I can explain to others how I am feeling. [SOA] 1 2 3 4 5 6

8. Hearing laughter makes me smile. [AR] 1 2 3 4 5 6

9. When I see a person experiencing a strong emotion, I can accurately assess what that person is feeling. [COG] 1 2 3 4 5 6

10. I am aware of other people's emotions. [SOA] 1 2 3 4 5 6

11. I believe that people who face discrimination have added stress that negatively impacts their lives. [MPT] 1 2 3 4 5 6

12. I am comfortable helping a person of a different race or   1 2 3 4 5 6
    ethnicity than my own. [MPT]

13. I take action to help others even if it does not personally   1 2 3 4 5 6
    benefit me. [MPT]

14. I believe government should protect the rights of minorities.   1 2 3 4 5 6
    [MPT]

15. I feel it is important to understand the political   1 2 3 4 5 6
    perspectives of people I don't agree with. [MPT]

The instrument contains 4 components: macro perspective-taking [MPT], cognitive empathy [COG], self-other awareness [SOA], and affective response [AR].

AR=3 items, SOA=3 items, COG=4, and MPT=5 items

Spanish Translation of the Empathy Assessment Index, the Social Empathy Index, and the Interpersonal and Social Empathy Index

▶ DAVID BECERRA AND MARÍA DEL ROSARIO
SILVA ARCINIEGA

WE ARE GRATEFUL TO OUR COLLEAGUES David Bercerra and María del Rosario Silva Arciniega for developing a Spanish-language translation of all the items for the Empathy Assessment Index (EAI), Social Empathy Index (SEI), and Interpersonal and Social Empathy Index (ISEI).

Items 1–22 correspond to the EAI. Items 1–40 correspond to the SEI. Items 1, 3, 4, 8, 9, 16, 18, 20, 21, 22, 27, 28, 29, 31, and 34 correspond to the ISEI.

1. Nunca (Never)
2. Casi nunca (Almost never/rarely)
3. A veces (Sometimes)
4. Frecuentemente (Frequently)
5. Casi siempre (Almost always)
6. Siempre (Always)

ÍNDICE DE EVALUACIÓN DE EMPATÍA PERSONAL Y SOCIAL

	CASI	A		CASI	
NUNCA	NUNCA	VECES	FRECUENTEMENTE	SIEMPRE	SIEMPRE
1	2	3	4	5	6

1. Cuando veo a alguien recibir un regalo que lo hace feliz, yo también me siento feliz.   1 2 3 4 5 6

2. Estabilidad emocional me describe bien.   1 2 3 4 5 6

3. Sé bien cómo entender las emociones de otras personas.   1 2 3 4 5 6

4. Puedo considerar mi punto de vista y la de otra persona al mismo tiempo.   1 2 3 4 5 6

5. Cuando me enojo, necesito mucho tiempo para que se me pase.   1 2 3 4 5 6

6. Puedo imaginar lo que el personaje está sintiendo en un buena película.   1 2 3 4 5 6

7. Cuando veo a alguien que sea humillado públicamente por otra persona me siento mal por él/ella.   1 2 3 4 5 6

8. Puedo reconocer la diferencia entre los sentimientos de otra persona y mis propios sentimientos.   1 2 3 4 5 6

9. Cuando veo una persona que demuestra una emoción fuerte, puedo evaluar con precisión lo que siente esa persona.   1 2 3 4 5 6

10. Mis amigos me ven como una persona temperamental.   1 2 3 4 5 6

11. Cuando veo a alguien que accidentalmente se golpea su pulgar con un martillo, yo mismo siento un destello de dolor.   1 2 3 4 5 6

12. Cuando veo a una persona que siente una emoción fuerte, puedo describir lo que esa persona siente a alguien más.   1 2 3 4 5 6

13. Puedo imaginar estar en la situación de otros.   1 2 3 4 5 6

14. Puedo distinguir la diferencia entre los sentimientos de mi amigo y mis sentimientos.   1 2 3 4 5 6

15. Considero los puntos de vista de otra gente en discusiones.   1 2 3 4 5 6

16. Cuando estoy con alguien que recibe noticias tristes, yo también me siento triste por un momento.   1 2 3 4 5 6

17. Cuando estoy molesto o infeliz, se me pasa pronto.   1 2 3 4 5 6

18. Puedo explicar a otros cómo me siento.   1 2 3 4 5 6

19. Puedo estar de acuerdo o en desacuerdo con otras personas.   1 2 3 4 5 6

20. Estoy consciente de lo que otros piensan de mí.   1 2 3 4 5 6

21. Escuchar risas me hace sonreír.   1 2 3 4 5 6

22. Estoy consciente de las emociones de otras personas.   1 2 3 4 5 6
23. Creo que los adultos que son pobres merecen asistencia social.   1 2 3 4 5 6
24. Lucho contra discriminación cuando la veo.   1 2 3 4 5 6
25. Creo que el gobierno debe de nivelar las condiciones para   1 2 3 4 5 6
    personas de diferentes grupos raciales/étnicos.
26. Creo que es necesario participar en servicio comunitario.   1 2 3 4 5 6
27. Creo que las personas que sufren discriminación tienen más   1 2 3 4 5 6
    estrés que impacta negativamente sus vidas.
28. Me siento cómodo ayudando a una persona de diferente raza   1 2 3 4 5 6
    o grupo étnico que la mía.
29. Tomo acción para ayudar a otros, aunque no me beneficie   1 2 3 4 5 6
    personalmente.
30. Puedo entender mejor a las personas que son diferentes de   1 2 3 4 5 6
    mí, aprendiendo de ellos directamente.
31. Creo que el gobierno debe proteger los derechos de todos los   1 2 3 4 5 6
    grupos en el país.
32. Creo que cada uno de nosotros debería participar en   1 2 3 4 5 6
    actividades políticas para beneficiar la sociedad.
33. Creo que la gente nacida en la pobreza tiene más obstáculos   1 2 3 4 5 6
    para lograr el bienestar económico que las personas que no
    nacieron en ella.
34. Creo que es importante entender las perspectivas políticas   1 2 3 4 5 6
    de las personas con las que no estoy de acuerdo.
35. Creo que es el derecho de todos los ciudadanos que tengan   1 2 3 4 5 6
    sus necesidades básicas.
36. Creo que el papel del gobierno es de actuar como árbitro,   1 2 3 4 5 6
    tomando decisiones que promueven la calidad de vida y el
    bienestar de la gente.
37. Me interesa entender por qué la gente no puede financiar sus   1 2 3 4 5 6
    necesidades básicas.
38. Yo creo que trabajando juntos, la gente puede cambiar la   1 2 3 4 5 6
    sociedad para que sea mejor para todos.
39. Creo que mis acciones afectarán a las próximas generaciones.   1 2 3 4 5 6
40. Creo que hay barreras en el sistema educativo de los Estados   1 2 3 4 5 6
    Unidos que impiden a algunos grupos de personas tener
    éxito económico.

REFERENCES

Almeida, P. R., Seixas, M. J., Ferreira-Santos, F., Vieira, J. B., Paiva, T. O., Moreira, P. S., & Costa, P. (2015). Empathic, moral, and antisocial outcomes associated with distinct components of psychopathy in healthy individuals: A Triarchic model approach. *Personality and Individual Differences, 85,* 205–211.

Arnsten, A. F. T. (2009). Stress signaling pathways that impair prefrontal cortex structure and function. *Nature Reviews, 10,* 410–422.

Asparouhov, T., & Bengt, M. (2012). Auxiliary variables in mixture modeling: A 3-step approach using Mplus. *Mplus Web Notes, 15,* 1–51.

Avenanti, A., Sirigu, A., & Aglioti, S. M. (2010). Racial bias reduces empathic sensorimotor resonance with other-race pain. *Current Biology, 20* (11), 1018–1022.

Baron-Cohen, S. (2011). *The science of evil: On empathy and the origins of cruelty.* New York: Basic Books.

Bassett, D. S., & Gazzaniga, M. S. (2011). Understanding complexity in the human brain. *Trends in Cognitive Sciences, 15* (5), 200–209.

Batson, C. D. (1991). *The altruism question: Toward a social-psychological answer.* Hillsdale, N.J.: Lawrence Erlbaum Associates.

——. (2011). These things called empathy: Eight related but distinct phenomena. In J. Decety & W. Ickes (Eds.), *The social neuroscience of empathy,* 3–15. Cambridge, Mass.: MIT Press.

——. (2012). The empathy-altruism hypothesis: Issues and implications. In J. Decety (Ed.), *Empathy from bench to bedside,* 41–54. Cambridge, Mass.: MIT Press.

Batson, C. D., Batson, J. G., Slingsby, J. K., Harrell, K. L., Peekna, H. M., & Todd, R. M. (1991). Empathic joy and the empathy-altruism hypothesis. *Journal of Personality and Social Psychology, 61,* 413–426.

Batson, C. D., Lishner, D. A., & Stocks, E. L. (2015). The empathy-altruism hypothesis. In D. A. Schroeder & W. G. Graziano (Eds.), *The Oxford handbook of prosocial behavior,* 259–281. New York: Oxford University Press.

Batson, C. D., Polycarpou, M. P., Harmon-Jones, E., Imhoff, H. J., Mitchener, E. C., Bednar, L. L., Klein, T. R., & Highberger, L. (1997). Empathy and attitudes: Can feeling for a member of a stigmatized group improve feelings toward the group? *Journal of Personality and Social Psychology, 72* (1), 105–118.

Batson, C. D., & Shaw, L. L. (1991). Evidence for altruism: Toward a pluralism of prosocial motives. *Psychological Inquiry, 2* (2), 107–122.

Bell, A.V., Richerson, P.J. & McElreath, R. (2009). Culture rather than genes provides greater scope for the evolution of large-scale human prosociality. *Proceedings of the National Academy of Sciences, 106* (42), 17671–17674.

Betti, V., & Aglioti, S. M. (2016). Dynamic construction of the neural networks underpinning empathy for pain. *Neuroscience and Behavioral Reviews, 63*, 191–206.

Blair, J., & White, S. F. (2013). Social cognition in individuals with psychopathic tendencies. In S. Baron-Cohen, H. Tager-Flusberg, & M. V. Lombardo (Eds.), *Understanding other minds: Perspectives from developmental social neuroscience*, 364–379. New York: Oxford University Press.

Blair, R. J. R. (2007). The amygdala and ventromedial prefrontal cortex in morality and psychopathy. *Trends in Cognitive Sciences, 11* (9), 387–392.

——. (2010). Psychopathy, frustration, and reactive aggression: The role of ventromedial prefrontal cortex. *British Journal of Psychology, 101*, 383–399.

Bowlby, J. (1969). *Attachment and loss*, Vol. 1, *Attachment*. New York: Basic Books.

Brewer, M. B. (1979). In-group bias in the minimal intergroup situation: A cognitive-motivational analysis. *Psychological Bulletin, 86* (2), 307–324.

Brown, K. W., & Ryan, R. M. (2003). The benefits of being present: Mindfulness and its role in psychological well-being. *Journal of Personality and Social Psychology, 84* (4), 822–848.

Brown, L. M., Bradley, M. M., & Lang, P. J. (2006). Affective reactions to pictures of ingroup and outgroup members. *Biological Psychology, 71* (3), 303–311.

Bucchioni, G., Lelard, T., Ahmaidi, S., Godefroy, O., Krystkowiak, P., & Mouras, H. (2015). Do we feel the same empathy for loved and hated peers? *PLoS ONE, 10* (5), 1–11.

Buruck, G., Wendsche, J., Melzer, M., Strobel, A., & Dörfel, D. (2014). Acute psychosocial stress and emotion regulation skills modulate empathic reactions to pain in others. *Frontiers in Psychology, 5*, article 517, 1–16.

Butters, R. P. (2010). *A meta-analysis of empathy training programs for client populations*. Ann Arbor, Mich.: ProQuest, UMI Dissertation Publishing.

Canale, S., Louis, D. Z., Maio, V., Wang, X., Rossi, G., Hojat, M., & Gonnella, J. S. (2012). The relationship between physician empathy and disease complications:

An empirical study of primary care physicians and their diabetic patients in Parma, Italy. *Academic Medicine, 87* (9), 1243–1249.

Carter, C. S., Harris, J., & Porges, S. W. (2011). Neural and evolutionary perspectives on empathy. In J. Decety & W. Ickes (Eds.), *The social neuroscience of empathy,* 169–182. Cambridge, Mass.: MIT Press.

Carter, C. S., & Porges, S. W. (2011). The neurobiology of social bonding and attachment. In J. Decety & J. T. Cacioppo (Eds.), *The Oxford handbook of social neuroscience,* 151–163. New York: Oxford University Press.

Chambers, J. R., & Davis, M. H. (2012). The role of the self in perspective-taking and empathy: Ease of self-simulation as a heuristic for inferring empathic feelings. *Social Cognition, 30,* 153–180.

Cherniss, C. (2010). Emotional intelligence: Toward clarification of a concept. *Industrial and Organizational Psychology, 3* (2), 110–126.

Chiao, J. Y. (2009). Cultural neuroscience: A once and future discipline. *Progress in Brain Research, 178,* 287–304.

———. (2011). Towards a cultural neuroscience of empathy and prosociality. *Emotion Review, 3* (1), 111–112.

Chiao, J. Y., & Blizinsky, K.D. (2010). Culture-gene coevolution of individualism-collectivism and the serotonin transporter gene. *Proceedings of the Royal Society B, 277,* 529–537.

Chiao, J. Y., & Mathur, V. A. (2010). Intergroup empathy: How does race affect empathic neural responses? *Current Biology, 20,* R478–R480.

Chiao, J. Y., Mathur, V. A., Harada, T., & Lipke, T. (2009). Neural basis of preference for human social hierarchy versus egalitarianism. *Annals of the New York Academy of Sciences, 1167,* 174–181.

Chlopan, B. E., McCain, M. L., Carbonell, J. L., & Hagen, R. L. (1985). Empathy: Review of available measures. *Journal of Personality and Social Psychology, 48* (3), 635–653.

Chung, R. C-Y., & Bemak, F. (2002). The relationship of culture and empathy in cross-cultural counseling. *Journal of Counseling and Development,* 80, 154–159.

Cikara, M., & Fiske, S. T. (2011). Bounded empathy: Neural responses to outgroup targets' (mis)fortunes. *Journal of Cognitive Neuroscience, 23* (12), 3791–3803.

Cliffordson, C. (2001). Parents' judgments and students' self-judgments of empathy. *European Journal of Psychological Assessment, 17* (1), 36–47.

Cole, P. M., Martin, S. E., & Dennis, T. A. (2004). Emotion regulation as a scientific construct: Methodological challenges and directions for child development research. *Child Development, 75* (2), 317–333.

Collins, N. L., & Feeney, B. C. (2000). A safe haven: An attachment theory perspective on support seeking and caregiving in intimate relationships. *Journal of Personality and Social Psychology, 78*, 1053–1073.

Conte, J. M. (2005). A review and critique of emotional intelligence measures. *Journal of Organizational Behavior, 26*, 433–440.

Coplan, A. (2011). Understanding empathy: Its features and effects. In A. Coplan & P. Goldie (Eds.), *Empathy: Philosophical and psychological perspectives*, 3–18. New York: Oxford University Press.

Coplan, A. & P. Goldie (Eds.) (2011). *Empathy: Philosophical and psychological perspectives*. New York: Oxford University Press.

Côté, S., Kraus, M. W., Cheng, B, Oveis, C., van der Löwe, I., Lian, H., & Keltner, D. (2011). Social power facilitates the effect of prosocial orientation on empathic accuracy. *Journal of Personality and Social Psychology, 101* (2), 217–232.

Covell, C. N., Huss, M. T., & Langhinrichsen-Rohling, J. (2007). Empathic deficits among male batterers: A multidimensional approach. *Journal of Family Violence, 22* (3), 165–174.

Crocker, L. D., Heller, W., Warren, S. L., O'Hare, A. J., Infantolino, Z. P., & Miller, G. A. (2013). Relationships among cognition, emotion, and motivation: Implications for intervention and neuroplasticity in psychopathology. *Frontiers in Human Neuroscience, 7*, article 261, 1–19.

Cuddy, A. J. C., Rock, M. S., & Norton, M. I. (2007). Aid in the aftermath of Hurricane Katrina: Inferences of secondary emotions and intergroup helping. *Group Processes & Intergroup Relations, 10* (1), 107–118.

Darwell, S. (1998). Empathy, sympathy, care. *Philosophical Studies, 89*, 261–282.

Davidov, M., Zahn-Walker, C., Roth-Hanania, R., & Knafo, A. (2013). Concern for others in the first year of life: Theory, evidence, and avenues for research. *Child Development Perspectives, 7* (2), 126–131.

Davidson, R. J., & Begley, S. (2012). *The emotional life of your brain: How its unique patterns affect the way you think, feel, and live—and how you can change them*. New York: Hudson Street Press.

Davidson, R. J., & McEwen, B. S. (2012). Social influences on neuroplasticity: Stress and interventions to promote well-being. *Nature Neuroscience, 15* (5), 689–695.

Davis, M. H. (1980). A multidimensional approach to individual differences in empathy. *JSAS Catalog of Selected Documents in Psychology, 10*, 85.

——. (1983). Measuring individual differences in empathy: Evidence for a multi-dimensional approach. *Journal of Personality and Social Psychology, 44* (1), 113–126.

——. (1996). *Empathy: A social psychological approach.* Boulder, Colo.: Westview Press.

——. (2015). Empathy and prosocial behavior. In D. A. Schroeder & W. G. Graziano (Eds.), *The Oxford handbook of prosocial behavior,* 282–306. New York: Oxford University Press.

De Dreu, C. K. W., & Kret, M. E. (2016). Oxytocin conditions intergroup relations through upregulated in-group empathy, cooperation, conformity, and defense. *Biological Psychiatry, 79* (3), 165–173.

de Vignemont, F. & Singer, T. (2006). The empathic brain: how, when and why? *Trends in Cognitive Sciences, 10* (10), 435–441.

de Waal, F. B. M. (2008). Putting the altruism back into altruism: The evolution of empathy. *Annual Review of Psychology, 59,* 279–300.

——. (2009). *The age of empathy: Nature's lessons for a kinder society.* New York: Random House.

——. (2012). The antiquity of empathy. *Science, 336,* 874–876.

Decety, J. (2005). Perspective taking as the royal avenue to empathy. In B. F. Malle & S. D. Hodges (Eds.), *Other minds: How humans bridge the divide between self and others,* 143–157. New York: Guilford Press.

——. (2010). The neurodevelopment of empathy in humans. *Developmental Neuroscience, 32,* 257–267.

——. (2011). Dissecting the neural mechanisms mediating empathy. *Emotion Review, 3* (1), 92–108.

——. (2015). The neural pathways, development, and functions of empathy. *Current Opinion in Behavioral Science, 3,* 1–6.

—— (Ed.). (2012). *Empathy: From bench to bedside.* Cambridge, Mass.: MIT Press.

Decety, J., Chen, C., Harenski, C., & Keihl, K. A. (2013). An fMRI study of affective perspective taking in individuals with psychopathy: Imagining another in pain does not evoke empathy. *Frontiers in Human Neuroscience, 7,* article 489, 1–12.

Decety, J., & Cowell, J. M. (2014). The complex relation between morality and empathy. *Trends in Cognitive Sciences, 18* (7), 337–339.

Decety, J., Echols, S., & Correll, J. (2009). The blame game: The effect of responsibility and social stigma on empathy for pain. *Journal of Cognitive Neuroscience, 22* (5), 985–997.

Decety, J., & Hodges, S. D. (2006). The social neuroscience of empathy. In P. A. M. Van Lange (Ed.), *Bridging social psychology: Benefits of transdisciplinary approaches*, 103–109. Mahwah, N.J.: Lawrence Erlbaum Associates.

Decety, J., & Jackson, P. L. (2004). The functional architecture of human empathy. *Behavioral and Cognitive Neuroscience Reviews, 3,* 71–100.

Decety, J., Jackson, P. L., & Brunet, E. (2007). The cognitive neuropsychology of empathy. In T. F. D. Farrow & P. W. R. Woodruff (Eds.), *Empathy in mental illness,* 239–260. Cambridge, UK: Cambridge University Press.

Decety, J., & Lamm, C. (2006). Human empathy through the lens of social neuroscience. *Scientific World Journal, 6,* 1146–1163.

——. (2011). Empathy versus personal distress: Recent evidence from social neuroscience. In J. Decety & W. Ickes (Eds.), *The social neuroscience of empathy.* Cambridge, Mass.: MIT Press.

Decety, J., & Meyer, M. (2008). From emotion resonance to empathic understanding: A social developmental neuroscience account. *Development and Psychopathology, 20,* 1053–1080.

Decety, J., & Michalska, K.J. (2012). How children develop empathy: The contribution of developmental affective neuroscience. In J. Decety (Ed.), *Empathy: From bench to bedside,* 167–190. Cambridge, Mass.: MIT Press.

Decety, J., & Moriguchi, Y. (2007). The empathic brain and its dysfunction in psychiatric populations: Implications for intervention across different clinical conditions. *BioPsychoSocial Medicine, 1* (22), 1–21.

Decety, J., & Skelly, L. R. (2014). The neural underpinnings of the experience of empathy: Lessons for psychopathy. In K. N. Ochsner & S. M. Kosslyn (Eds.), *The Oxford handbook of cognitive neuroscience, Volume 2: The cutting edges,* 228–243. New York: Oxford University Press.

Decety, J., & Sommerville, J. A. (2003). Shared representations between self and other: A social cognitive neuroscience view. *Trends in Cognitive Sciences, 7* (12), 527–533.

Decety, J., Yang, C-Y., & Cheng, Y. (2010). Physicians down-regulate their pain empathy response: An event-related brain potential study. *NeuroImage, 50,* 1676–1682.

DeTurk, S. (2001). Intercultural empathy: Myth, competency, or possibility for alliance building? *Communication Education, 50* (4), 374–384.

Deutsch, F., & Madle, R. (1975). Empathy: Historic and current conceptualizations, measurement, and a cognitive theoretical perspective. *Human Development, 18,* 267–287.

Dodge, T. (2013). *Iraq: From war to a new authoritarianism.* New York: Routledge. http://dx.doi.org/10.1146%2Fannurev.psych.59.103006.093625

Dondi, M., Simion, F., & Caltran, G. (1999). Can newborns discriminate between their own cry and the cry of another newborn infant? *Developmental Psychology, 35,* 418–426.

Drwecki, B. B., Moore, C. F., Ward, S. E., & Prkachin, K. M. (2011). Reducing racial disparities in pain treatment: The role of empathy and perspective-taking. *Pain, 152,* 1001–1006.

Dunfield, K., Kulmeier, V. A., O'Connell, L., & Kelly, E. (2011). Examining the diversity of prosocial behavior: Helping, sharing, and comforting in infancy. *Infancy, 16* (3), 227–247.

Dvash, J., & Shamay-Tsoory, S. G. (2014). Theory of mind and empathy as multi-dimensional constructs: Neurological foundations. *Topics in Language Disorders, 34* (4), 282–295.

Dyche, L., & Zayas, L. H. (2001). Cross-cultural empathy and training the con-temporary psychotherapist. *Clinical Social Work Journal, 29,* 3, 245–258.

Einolf, C. J. (2008). Empathic concern and prosocial behaviors: A test of experimen-tal results using survey data. *Social Science Research, 37,* 1267–1279.

Eisenberg, N. (1986). *Altruistic emotion, cognition, and behavior.* Hillsdale, N.J.: Lawrence Erlbaum Associates.

——. (2002). Distinctions among various modes of empathy-related reactions: A matter of importance in humans. *Behavioral and Brain Sciences, 25* (1), 33–34.

Eisenberg, N., Eggum, N. D., & Di Gunta, L. (2010). Empathy-related responding: Associations with prosocial behavior, aggression, and intergroup relations. *Social Issues and Policy Review, 4* (1), 143–180.

Eisenberg, N., Eggum-Wilkens, N. D., & Spinrad, T. L. (2015). The development of prosocial behavior. In D. A. Schroeder & W. G. Graziano (Eds.), *The Oxford handbook of prosocial behavior,* 114–136. New York: Oxford University Press.

Eisenberg, N., & Fabes, R. A. (1998). Prosocial development. In W. Damon (Ed.), *Handbook of child psychology,* 5th ed., Vol. 3, N. Eisenberg (Ed), *Social, emotional, and personality development,* 701–778. New York: Wiley.

Eisenberg, N., Fabes, R. A., Bustamante, D., Mathy, R. M., Miller, P. A., & Lindholm, E. (1988). Differentiation of vicariously induced emotional reactions in children. *Developmental Psychology, 24* (2), 237–246.

Eisenberg, N., Fabes, R. A., Schaller, M., Miller, P., & Carlo, G. (1991). Personality and socialization correlates of vicarious emotional responding. *Journal of Personality and Social Psychology, 61* (3), 459–470.

Eisenberg, N. & Lennon, R. (1983). Sex differences in empathy and related capacities. *Psychological Bulletin, 94,* 100–131.

Eisenberg, N., Smith, C. L., Sadovsky, A., & Spinrad, T. L. (2004). Effortful control: Relations with emotion regulation, adjustment, and socialization in childhood. In R. F. Baumeister & K. D. Vohs (Eds.), *Handbook of self-regulation: Research, theory, and applications,* 259–282. New York: Guilford Press.

Elsegood, K. J., & Duff, S. C. (2010). Theory of mind in men who have sexually offended against children. *Sexual Abuse: A Journal of Research and Treatment, 22* (1), 112–131.

Engelen, E-M., & Röttger-Rössler, B. (2012). Current disciplinary and interdisciplinary debates on empathy. *Emotion Review, 4* (1), 3–8.

Eres, R., Decety, J., Louis, W. R., & Molenberghs, P. (2015). Individual differences in local gray matter density are associated with differences in affective and cognitive empathy. *NeuroImage, 117,* 305–310.

Eres, R., & Molenberghs, P. (2013). The influence of group membership on the neural correlates involved in empathy. *Frontiers in Human Neuroscience, 7,* article 176, 1–6.

Evans, G. W., & Fuller-Rowell, E. (2013). Childhood poverty, chronic stress, and young adult working memory: The protective role of self-regulatory capacity. *Developmental Science, 16* (5), 688–696.

Evans, G. W. & Schamberg, M.A. (2009). Childhood poverty, chronic stress, and adult working memory. *Proceedings of the National Academy of Sciences,* 106 (16), 6545–6549.

Ewen, B. S. (2009). Stress and coping. In G. G. Berntson & J. T. Cacioppo (Eds.), *Handbook of neuroscience for the behavioral sciences,* 2: 1220–1235. Hoboken, N.J.: John Wiley & Sons.

Fawley-King, K., & Merz, E. C. (2014). Effects of child maltreatment on brain development. In H.C. Matto, J. Strolin-Goltzman, & M. S. Ballan (Eds.), *Neuroscience for social work: Current research and practice,* 111–139. New York: Springer.

Feshbach, N. D., & Roe, K. (1968). Empathy in six- and seven-year-olds. *Child Development, 39,* 133–145.

Feygina, I., & Henry, P. J. (2015). Culture and prosocial behavior. In D. A. Schroeder & W. G. Graziano, *The Oxford handbook of prosocial behavior,* 188–208. New York: Oxford University Press.

Fiske, S. T. (2009). From dehumanization and objectification to rehumanization: Neuroimaging studies on the building blocks of empathy. In S. Atran, A. Navarro, K. Ochsner, A. Tobeña, & O. Vilarroya (Eds.), *Values, empathy, and fairness across social barriers*, 31–34. Boston, Mass.: Blackwell.

Fonagy, P., Gergely, G., Jurist, E., & Target, M. (2004). *Affect regulation, mentalization, and the development of the self.* New York: Other Press.

Frank, R. H. (2001). Cooperation through emotional commitment. In R. M. Nesse (Ed.), *Evolution and the capacity for commitment*, 57–76. New York: Russell Sage Foundation.

Frith, C. D., & Frith, U. (2006). The neural basis of mentalizing. *Neuron, 50* (4), 531–534.

Galinsky, A. D., Ku, G., & Wang, C. S. (2005). Perspective-taking and self-other overlap: Fostering social bonds and facilitating social coordination. *Group Processes & Intergroup Relations, 8* (2), 109–124.

Galinsky, A.D., Magee, J. C., Inesi, M. E., & Gruenfeld, D. H. (2006). Power and perspectives not taken. *Psychological Science, 17* (12), 1068–1074.

Galinsky, A. D., & Moskowitz, G. B. (2000). Perspective-taking: Decreasing stereotype expression, stereotype accessibility, and in-group favoritism. *Journal of Personality and Social Psychology, 28*, 708–724.

Gallese, V. (2007). Before and below 'theory of mind': Embodied simulation and the neural correlates of social cognition. *Philosophical Transactions of the Royal Society of Britain, 362*, 659–669.

——. (2014). Mirror neurons and the perception-action link. In K. N. Ochsner & S. M. Kosslyn (Eds.), *The Oxford handbook of cognitive neuroscience, Vol. 2: The cutting edges*, 244–256. New York: Oxford University Press.

Garnefski, N., & Kraaji, V. (2006). Cognitive emotion regulation questionnaire— Development of a short 18-item version (CERQ-Short). *Personality and Individual Differences, 41*, 1045–1053.

Gentili, C., Cristea, I. A., Ricciardi, E., Costescu, C., David, D., & Pietrini, P. (2015). Neurobiological correlates of the attitude toward human empathy. *Rivista Internazionale di Filosofia e Psicologia, 6*, 1, 70–87.

Gerdes, K. E. (2011). Empathy, sympathy, and pity: 21st-century definitions and implications for practice and research. *Journal of Social Service Research, 37* (1), 230–241.

Gerdes, K. E., Geiger, J. M., Lietz, C. A., Wagaman, M. A., & Segal, E. A. (2012). Examination of known-groups validity for the Empathy Assessment Index (EAI): Differences in EAI scores between social service providers and recipients at community treatment agencies. *Journal of the Society for Social Work Research*, 3 (2), 94–112.

Gerdes, K. E., Lietz, C. A., & Segal, E. A. (2011). Measuring empathy in the twenty-first century: The development of an empathy index rooted in social cognitive neuroscience and social justice. *Social Work Research*, *35* (2), 83–93.

Gerdes, K. E., & Segal, E. A. (2009). A social work model of empathy. *Advances in Social Work*, *10* (2), 114–127.

——. (2011). The importance of empathy for social work practice: Integrating new science. *Social Work*, *56* (2), 141–148.

Gerdes, K. E., Segal, E. A., & Lietz, C. A. (2010). Conceptualising and measuring empathy: The need for clarity and consistency. *British Journal of Social Work*, *40* (7), 2326–2343.

Gerdes, K. E., Segal, E. A., & Harmon, J. K. (2014). Your brain on empathy: Implications for social work practice. In H. C. Matto, J. Strolin-Goltzman, & M. S. Ballan (Eds.), *Neuroscience for social work: Current research and practice*, 9–36. New York: Springer.

Gerdes, K. E., Segal, E. A., Jackson, K. F., & Mullins, J. L. (2011). Teaching empathy: A model rooted in social cognitive neuroscience and social justice. *Journal of Social Work Education*, *47* (1), 109–131.

Gianaros, P. J., Manuck, S. B., Sheu, L. K., Kuan, D. C. H., Votruba-Drzal, E., Craig, A. E., & Hariri, A.R. (2011). Parental education predicts corticostriatal functionality in adulthood. *Cerebral Cortex*, *21* (4), 896–910.

Gilbert, D. T., & Malone, P. S. (1995). The correspondence bias. *Psychological Bulletin*, *117* (1), 21–38.

Gini, G., Albiero, P., Benelli, B., & Altoe, G. (2008). Determinants of adolescents' active defending and passive bystanding behavior in bullying. *Journal of Adolescence*, *31*, 93–105.

Gleichgerrcht, E., & Decety, J. (2012). The costs of empathy among health professionals. In J. Decety (Ed.), *Empathy from bench to bedside*, 245–261. Cambridge, Mass.: MIT Press.

Glick, P. (2005). Choice of scapegoats. In J. F. Dovidio, P. Glick, & L. A. Rudman (Eds.), *On the nature of prejudice: 50 years after Allport*, 244–261. Malden, Mass.: Blackwell.

——. (2008). When neighbors blame neighbors: Scapegoating and the breakdown of ethnic relations. In V. M. Esses & R. A. Vernon (Eds.), *Explaining the breakdown of ethnic relations*, 123–146. Malden, Mass.: Blackwell.

Glick, P., & Paluck, E. L. (2013). The aftermath of genocide: History as a proximal cause. *Journal of Social Issues, 69* (1), 200–208.

Goetz, J. I., Keltner, D., & Simon-Thomas, E. (2010). Compassion: An evolutionary analysis and empirical review. *Psychological Bulletin, 136* (3), 351–374.

Goldman, A. I. (2011). Two routes to empathy: Insights from cognitive neuroscience. In A. Coplan & P. Goldie (Eds.), *Empathy: Philosophical and psychological perspectives*, 31–44. New York: Oxford University Press.

Goleman, D. (1994). *Emotional intelligence: Why it can matter more than IQ.* New York: Bantam.

———. *Social intelligence: The new science of human relationships.* New York: Bantam Books.

Gouin, J-P., Hantsoo, L. V., & Kiecolt-Glaser, J. K. (2011). Stress, negative emotions, and inflammation. In J. Decety & J. T. Cacioppo (Eds.), *The Oxford handbook of social neuroscience*, 814–829. New York: Oxford University Press.

Gu, X., Gao, Z., Wang, X., Liu, X., Knight, R. T., Hof, P. R., & Fan, J. (2012). Anterior insular cortex is necessary for empathetic pain perception. *Brain*, 135, 2726–2735.

Gutsell, J. N., & Inzlicht, M. (2010). Empathy constrained: Prejudice predicts reduced mental simulation of actions during observations of outgroups. *Journal of Experimental Social Psychology, 46*, 841–845.

———. (2012). Intergroup differences in the sharing of emotive states: Neural evidence of an empathy gap. *Social Cognitive and Affective Neuroscience, 7* (5), 596–603.

Hackney, H. (1978). The evolution of empathy. *Personnel and Guidance Journal, 57* (1), 35–38.

Haidt, J. (2012). *The righteous mind: Why good people are divided by politics and religion.* New York: Random House.

Hamilton, W. D. (1964). The genetic evolution of social behavior. *Journal of Theoretical Biology, 7* (parts 1 & 2), 1–52.

Harris, L. T., & Fiske, S. T. (2006). Dehumanizing the lowest of the low: Neuroimaging responses to extreme out-groups. *Psychological Science, 17* (10), 847–853.

———. (2011). Perceiving humanity or not: A social neuroscience approach to dehumanized perception. In A. Todorov, S. T. Fiske, & D. A. Prentice (Eds.), *Social neuroscience: Toward understanding the underpinnings of the social mind*, 123–134. New York: Oxford University Press.

Harris, P. L. (2000). Understanding emotion. In M. Levin & J. M. Haviland-Jones (Eds), *Handbook of emotions*, 281–292. New York: Guilford Press.

Hatfield, E., Rapson, R. L., & Le, Y-C. L. (2011). Emotional contagion and empathy. In J. Decety & W. Ickes (Eds.), *The social neuroscience of empathy*, 19–30. Cambridge, Mass.: MIT Press.

Hein, G., Silani, G., Preuschoff, K., Batson, C. D., & Singer, T. (2010). Neural responses to ingroup and outgroup members' suffering predict individual differences in costly helping. *Neuron, 68*, 149–160.

Heinrichs, M., Chen, F. S., & Domes, G. (2013). Social neuropeptides in the human brain: Oxytocin and social behavior. In S. Baron-Cohen, H. Tager-Flusberg, & M. V. Lombardo (Eds.), *Understanding other minds*, 291–307. New York: Oxford University Press.

Hetu, S., Taschereau-Dumouchel, V., & Jackson, P. L. (2012). Stimulating the brain to study social interactions and empathy. *Brain Stimulation, 5*, 95–102.

Hickok, G. (2008). Eight problems for the mirror neuron theory of action understanding in monkeys and humans. *Journal of Cognitive Neuroscience, 21* (7), 1229–1243.

Hodges, S. D., & Wegner, D. M. (1997). Automatic and controlled empathy. In W. Ickes (Ed.), *Empathic Accuracy*, 311–339. New York: Guilford Press.

Hoffman, M. L. (1981). Is altruism part of human nature? *Journal of Personality and Social Psychology, 40* (1), 121–137.

——. (2000). *Empathy and moral development: Implications for caring and justice.* London: Cambridge University Press.

——. (2011). Empathy, justice, and the law. In A. Coplan & P. Goldie (Eds.), *Empathy: Philosophical and psychological perspectives*, 230–254. New York: Oxford University Press.

Hogan, R. (1969). Development of an empathy scale. *Journal of Consulting and Clinical Psychology, 33* (3), 307–316.

Hogeveen, J., Inzlicht, M., & Obhi, S. S. (2014). Power changes how the brain responds to others. *Journal of Experimental Psychology, 143* (2), 755–762.

Hollan, D. (2012). Emerging issues in the cross-cultural study of empathy. *Emotion Review, 4* (1), 70–78.

Howell, J. L. & Shepperd, J. A. (2011). Demonstrating the correspondence bias. *Teaching of Psychology, 38* (4), 243–246.

Iacoboni, M. (2008). *Mirroring people: The new science of how we connect with others.* New York: Farrar, Straus & Giroux.

——. (2009). Imitation, empathy, and mirror neurons. *Annual Review of Psychology*, *60*, 653–670.

——. (2011). Within each other: Neural mechanisms for empathy in primate brains. In A. Coplan & P. Goldie (Eds.), *Empathy: Philosophical and psychological perspectives*, 45–57. New York: Oxford University Press.

Iacoboni, M., Molnar-Szakacs, I., Gallese, V., Buccino, G., Mazziotta, J. C., & Rizzolatti, G. (2005). Grasping the intentions of others with one's own mirror neuron system. *PLoS Biology, 3* (3), 529–535.

Ickes, W., Gesn, P. R., & Graham, T. (2000). Gender differences in empathic accuracy: Differential ability or differential motivation? *Personal Relationships, 7,* 95–109.

Jackson, P. L., Brunet, E., Meltzoff, A. N., & Decety, J. (2006). Empathy examined through the neural mechanisms involved in imagining how I feel versus how you feel pain: An event-related fMRI study. *Neuropsychologia, 44,* 752–761.

Jensen, P., Weersing, R., Hoagwood, K. E., & Goldman, E. (2005). What is evidence for evidence-based treatments? A hard look at our soft underbelly. *Mental Health Services Research, 7* (1), 53–74.

Jolliffe, D., & Farrington, D. P. (2004). Empathy and offending: A systematic review and meta-analysis. *Aggression and Violent Behavior, 9* (5), 441–476.

Jolliffe, D., & Farrington, D. P. (2006). Development and validation of the Basic Empathy Scale. *Journal of Adolescence, 29,* 589–611.

Kaplan, J. T., & Iacoboni, M. (2006). Getting a grip on other minds: Mirror neurons, intention understanding, and cognitive empathy. *Social Neuroscience, 1* (3/4), 175–183.

Kasl, E., & Yorks, L. (2016). Do I really know you? Do you really know me? Empathy amid diversity in differing learning contexts. *Adult Education Quarterly, 66* (1), 3–20.

Keenan, J. P., Oh, H., & Amati, F. (2011). An overview of self-awareness and the brain. In J. Decety & J. T. Cacioppo (Eds.), *The Oxford handbook of social neuroscience*, 314–324. New York: Oxford University Press.

Keltner, D. (2010). The compassionate instinct. In D. Keltner, J. Marsh & J. A. Smith (Eds.), *The compassionate instinct*, 8–15. New York: Norton.

Kersting, A., Ohrmann, P., Pedersen, A., Kroker, K., Samberg, D., & Bauer, J. (2009). Neural activation underlying acute grief in women after the loss of an unborn child. *American Journal of Psychiatry, 166,* 1402–1410.

Kim, J., & Cicchetti, D. (2009). Longitudinal pathways linking child maltreatment, emotion regulation, peer relations, and psychopathology. *Journal of Child Psychology and Psychiatry, 51* (6), 706–716.

Koster-Hale, J., & Saxe, R. (2013). Functional neuroimaging of theory of mind. In S. Baron-Cohen, H. Tager-Flushing, & M. V. Lombardo (Eds.), *Understanding other minds: Perspectives from developmental social neuroscience,* 132–163. New York: Oxford University Press.

Kraus, M. W., Côté, S., & Keltner, D. (2010). Social class, contextualism, and empathic accuracy. *Psychological Science, 21* (11), 1716–1723.

Kraus, M. W., Piff, P. K., & Keltner, D. (2009). Social class, sense of control, and social explanation. *Journal of Personality and Social Psychology, 97,* 992–1004.

——. (2011). Social class as culture: The convergence of resources and rank in the social realm. *Current Directions in Psychological Science, 20* (4), 246–250.

Krendl, A. C., & Heatherton, T. F. (2009). Self versus others/self-regulation. In G. G. Berntson & J. T. Cacioppo (Eds.), *Handbook of neuroscience for the behavioral sciences,* 2:859–878. Hoboken, N.J.: John Wiley.

Laible, D. J., Carlo, G., & Roesch, S. C. (2004). Pathways to self-esteem in late adolescence: The role of parent and peer attachment, empathy, and social behaviours. *Journal of Adolescence, 27,* 703–716.

Lamm, C., Batson, C. D., & Decety, J. (2007). The neural substrate of human empathy: Effects of perspective-taking and cognitive appraisal. *Journal of Cognitive Neuroscience, 19* (1), 42–58.

Lamm, C., Bukowski, H., & Silani, G. (2016). From shared to distinct self-other representations in empathy: Evidence from neurotypical function and sociocognitive disorders. *Philosophical Transactions of the Royal Society B, 371* (1686), 20150083.

Lamm, C., & Majdandžić, J. (2015). The role of shared neural activations, mirror neurons, and morality in empathy—A critical comment. *Neuroscience Research, 90,* 15–24.

Lamm, C., Meltzoff, A. N., & Decety, J. (2009). How do we empathize with someone who is not like us? A functional magnetic resonance imaging study. *Journal of Cognitive Neuroscience, 22* (2), 362–276.

Lamm, C., Nusbaum, H. C., Meltzoff, A. N., & Decety, J. (2007). What are you feeling? Using functional magnetic resonance imaging to assess the modulation of sensory and affective responses during empathy for pain. *PLoS ONE, 12,* (e1292), 1–16.

Lamm, C., Silani, G., & Singer, T. (2015). Distinct neural networks underlying empathy for pleasant and unpleasant touch. *Cortex, 70,* 79–89.

Layous, K., Nelson, S. K., Oberle, E., Schonert-Reichl, K. A., & Lyubomirsky, S. (2012). Kindness counts: Prompting prosocial behavior in preadolescents boosts peer acceptance and well-being. *PLoS ONE, 7* (12), e51380.

Leibovich, M. (2015, October 4). Donald Trump is not going anywhere. *New York Times Sunday Magazine,* 28.

Lietz, C. A. (2011). Empathic action and family resilience: A narrative examination of the benefits of helping others. *Journal of Social Service Research, 37* (3), 254–265.

Lietz, C. A., Gerdes, K. E., Sun, F., Geiger, J. M., Wagaman, M. A., & Segal, E. A. (2011). The Empathy Assessment Index (EAI): A confirmatory factor analysis of a multidimensional model of empathy. *Journal of the Society for Social Work Research, 2* (2), 104–124.

Lipps, T. (1903). Einfühlung, inner Nachahmung, und Organaempfindaungen. *Archiv für die gesamte psychologie, 1,* 465–519. Translated as "Empathy, inner imitation, and sense-feelings." In M. Rader (Ed.), (1979), *A modern book of esthetics,* 374–382. New York: Holt, Rinehart, & Winston.

Lupien, S. J., McEwen, B. S., Gunnar, M. R., & Heim, C. (2009). Effects of stress throughout the lifespan on the brain, behavior, and cognition. *Nature, 10,* 434–445.

Mahabharata (n.d.). Anusasana Parva, Book 13, section CXIII. Available at http://www.mahabharataonline.com/translation/mahabharata_13b078.php.

Marsh, A. A., Finger, E. C., Fowler, K. A., Jurkowitz, I. T. N., Schechter, J. C., Yu, H. H., Pine, D. S., & Blair, R. J. R. (2011). Reduced amygdala-orbitofrontal connectivity during moral judgments in youths with disruptive behavior disorders and psychopathic traits. *Psychiatry Research: Neuroimaging, 194,* 279–286.

Martin, G. B., & Clark, R. D. (1987). Distress crying in neonates: Species and peer specificity. *Developmental Psychology, 18,* 3–9.

Mathur, V. A., Harada, T., Lipke, T., & Chiao, J. Y. (2010). Neural basis of extraordinary empathy and altruistic motivation. *NeuroImage, 51* (4), 1468–1475.

Mayberry, M. L., & Espelage, D. L. (2007). Associations among empathy, social competence, & reactive/proactive aggression subtypes. *Journal of Youth and Adolescence, 36* (6), 787–798.

Mayo Clinic. (2014, May). Oxytocin: The social hormone. *Health Letter,* 6. Rochester, MN: Author.

McCall, C., & Singer, T. (2013). Empathy and the brain. In S. Baron-Cohen, H. Tager-Flusberg, & M. V. Lombardo (Eds.), *Understanding other minds: Perspectives from developmental social neuroscience*, 195–213. New York: Oxford University Press.

Mehrabian, A., & Epstein, N. (1972). A measure of emotional empathy. *Journal of Personality, 40* (40), 525–543.

Meltzoff, A. N., & Moore, M. K. (1994). Imitation, memory, and the representation of persons. *Infant Behavior and Development, 17* (1), 83–99.

Meyer, M. L., Masten, C. L., Ma, Y., Wang, C., Shi, Z., Eisenberger, N. I., & Han, S. (2012). Empathy for the social suffering of friends and strangers recruits distinct patterns of brain activation. *Social Cognitive and Affective Neuroscience, 8* (4), 446–454.

Meyer-Lindenberg, A., & Tost, H. (2012). Neural mechanisms of social risk for psychiatric disorders. *Nature Nuroscience, 15* (5), 663–668.

Mikulincer, M., Gillath, O., Halevy, V., Avihou, N., Avidan, S., & Eshkoli, N. (2001). Attachment theory and reaction to others' needs: Evidence that activation of the sense of attachment security promotes empathic responses. *Journal of Personality and Social Psychology, 81* (6), 1205–1224.

Mikulincer, M., Shaver, P. R., Gillath, O., & Nitzberg, R. A. (2005). Attachment, caregiving, and altruism: Boosting attachment security increases compassion and helping. *Journal of Personality and Social Psychology, 89* (5), 817–839.

Mikulincer, M., & Shaver, P. R. (2015). An attachment perspective on prosocial attitudes and behavior. In D. A. Schroeder & W. G. Graziano (Eds.), *The Oxford handbook of prosocial behavior*, 209–230. New York: Oxford University Press.

Mitchell, J. P. (2009). Inferences about mental states. *Philosophical Transactions of the Royal Society Biological Sciences, 364*, 1309–1316.

Moran, J. M., Kelley, W. M., & Heatherton, T. F. (2014). Self-knowledge. In K. N. Ochsner & S. M. Kosslyn (Eds.), *The Oxford handbook of cognitive neuroscience*, Vol. 2: *The cutting edges*, 135–147. New York: Oxford University Press.

Morin, A. (2004). A neurocognitive and socioecological model of self-awareness. *Genetic, Social, and General Psychology Monographs, 103*, 197–222.

Morrell, M. E. (2010). *Empathy and democracy: Feeling, thinking, and deliberation.* University Park: Pennsylvania State University Press.

Müller, B. C. N., Maaskant, A. J., van Baaren, R. B., & Dijksterhuis, A. (2012). Prosocial consequences of imitation. *Psychological Reports, 110* (3), 891–898.

Murphy, B., Shepard, S., Eisenberg, N., Fabes, R., & Guthrie, I. (1999). Contemporaneous and longitudinal relations of dispositional empathy to emotionality, regulation, and social functioning. *Journal of Early Adolescence, 19*, 66–97.

Nadler, A. (2010). Interpersonal and intergroup helping relations as power relations. In S. Stürmer & M. Snyder (Eds.), *The psychology of prosocial behavior*, 269–287. West Sussex, U.K.: Wiley-Blackwell.

National Scientific Council on the Developing Child. (2014). *Excessive stress disrupts the architecture of the developing brain*. Working Paper 3. Cambridge, Mass.: Center on the Developing Child at Harvard University.

Obama, B. (2013). Remarks by the President at Morehouse College commencement ceremony. http://www.whitehouse.gov/the-press-office/2013/05/19/remarks-president-morehouse-college-commencement-ceremony.

O'Brien, E., & Ellsworth, P. C. (2012). More than skin deep: Visceral states are not projected onto dissimilar others. *Psychological Science, 23* (4), 391–396.

Park, H-J., & Friston, K. (2013). Structural and functional brain networks: From connections to cognition. *Science, 342* (1), 579–587.

Paus, T. (2011). Brain development during childhood and adolescence. In J. Decety & J. T. Cacioppo (Eds.), *The Oxford handbook of social neuroscience*, 293–313. New York: Oxford University Press.

Pedersen, R. (2009). Empirical research on empathy in medicine: A critical review. *Patient Education and Counseling, 76*, 307–322.

Pessoa, L. (2014). Understanding brain networks and brain organization. *Physics of Life Reviews, 11* (30), 400–435.

Phillips, K. F. V. & Power, M. J. (2007). A new self-report measure of emotion regulation in adolescents: The regulation of emotions questionnaire. *Clinical Psychology and Psychotherapy, 14*, 145–156.

Pinker, S. (2011). *The better angels of our nature: Why violence has declined*. New York: Viking.

Pithers, W. (1999). Empathy: Definition, enhancement, and relevance to the treatment of sexual abusers. *Journal of Interpersonal Violence, 14* (3), 257–284.

Preston, S. D., & de Waal, F. B. M. (2002). Empathy: Its ultimate and proximate bases. *Behavioral and Brain Sciences, 25*, 1–72.

——. (2011). Altruism. In J. Decety & J. T. Cacioppo (Eds.), *The Oxford handbook of social neuroscience*, 565–585. New York: Oxford University Press.

Preston, S. D., & Hofelich, A. J. (2012). The many faces of empathy: Parsing empathic phenomena through a proximate, dynamic-systems view of representing the other in the self. *Emotion Review, 4* (1), 24–33.

Prinz, J. J. (2011). Is empathy necessary for morality? In A. Coplan & P. Goldie (Eds.), *Empathy: Philosophical and psychological perspectives*, 211–229. New York: Oxford University Press.

Pryor, J. B., Reeder, G. D., Monroe, A. E., & Patel, A. (2010). Stigmas and prosocial behavior: Are people reluctant to help stigmatized persons? In S. Stürmer & M. Snyder (Eds.), *The psychology of prosocial behavior*, 59–80. West Sussex, U.K.: Wiley-Blackwell.

Putnam, R. D. (1993). *Making democracy work*. Princeton, N.J.: Princeton University Press.

Reniers, R. L. E. P., Corcoran, R., Drake, R., Shryane, N. M., & Völlm, B. A. (2011). The QCAE: A questionnaire of cognitive and affective empathy. *Journal of Personality Assessment, 93* (1), 84–95.

Rifkin, J. (2009). *The empathic civilization: The race to global consciousness in a world in crisis*. New York: Penguin.

Righetti, F., Hofmann, W., Gere, J., Visserman, M. L., & Van Lange, P. A. M. (2016, March 7). The burden of empathy: Partners' responses to divergence of interests in daily life. *Emotion*, advance online publication. http//dx.doi.org /10.1037/emo0000163.

Rizzolatti, G., & Craighero, L. (2004). The mirror neuron system. *Annual Review of Neuroscience, 27*, 169–192.

Rizzolatti, G., Fabbri-Destro, M., & Cattaneo, L. (2009). Mirror neurons and their clinical relevance. *Nature Clinical Practice Neurology, 5* (1), 24–34.

Roan, L., Strong, B., Foss, P., Yager, M., Gehlbach, H., & Metcalf, K. A. (2009). *Social perspective taking*. Technical Report 1259. Arlington, Va.: U.S. Army Research Institute for the Behavioral and Social Sciences.

Robbins, T. G., & DiDomenica, P. J. (2013). *Journey from Genesis to genocide: Hate, empathy and the plight of humanity*. Pittsburgh: Dorrance.

Rodkinson, M.L. (1903). *The Babylonian Talmud, Book 1: Tract Sabbath*. Available at www.sacred-texts/jud/t01/t0110.htm.

Rogers, C. R. (1957). The necessary and sufficient conditions of therapeutic personality change. *Journal of Consulting Psychology, 21*, 95–103.

Rumble, A. C., Van Lange, P. A. M., & Parks, C. (2010). The benefits of empathy: When empathy may sustain cooperation in social dilemmas. *European Journal of Social Psychology, 40*, 856–866.

Sagi, A., & Hofman, M. L. (1976). Empathic distress in the newborn. *Developmental Psychology, 12*, 175–176.

Sapolsky, R. M. (2004). *Why zebras don't get ulcers: The acclaimed guide to stress, stress-related diseases, and coping*, 3rd ed. New York: St. Martin's Griffin.

Saxe, R. (2006). Four brain regions for one Theory of Mind? In J. T. Cacioppo, P. S. Visser, & C. L. Pickett (Eds.), *Social neuroscience: People thinking about thinking people*, 83–101. Cambridge, Mass.: MIT Press.

Schnell, K., Bluschke, S., Konradt, B., & Walter, H. (2011). Functional relations of empathy and mentalizing: An fMRI study on the neural basis of cognitive empathy. *NeuroImage, 54*, 1743–1754.

Schulte-Rüther, M., Markowitsch, H. J., Shah, N. J., Fink, G. R., & Piefke, M. (2008). Gender differences in brain networks supporting empathy. *NeuroImage, 42*, 393–403.

Segal, E. A. (2006). Welfare as we *should* know it: Social empathy and welfare reform. In K. M. Kilty, & E. A. Segal, (Eds.), *The promise of welfare reform: Rhetoric or reality?*, 265–274. Binghamton, N.Y.: Haworth Press.

——. (2007). Social empathy: A tool to address the contradiction of working but still poor. *Families in Society: The Journal of Contemporary Social Sciences, 88* (3), 333–337.

——. (2011). Social empathy: A model built on empathy, contextual understanding, and social responsibility that promotes social justice. *Journal of Social Service Research, 37* (1), 266–277.

——. (2014). Social empathy. In C. Franklin (Ed.). *The encyclopedia of social work online*. New York: Oxford University Press and the National Association of Social Workers. DOI: 10.1093/acrefore/9780199975839.013.1152.

Segal, E. A., Cimino, A. N., Gerdes, K. E., Harmon, J. K., & Wagaman, M. A. (2013). A confirmatory factor analysis of the Interpersonal and Social Empathy Index. *Journal of the Society for Social Work and Research, 4* (3), 131–153.

Segal, E. A., & Wagaman, M. A. (in press). Social empathy as a framework for teaching social justice. *Journal of Social Work Education*.

Segal, E. A., Wagaman, M. A., & Gerdes, K. E. (2012). Developing the Social Empathy Index: An exploratory factor analysis. *Advances in Social Work, 13* (3), 542–60.

Shamay-Tsoory, S. G. (2011). The neural bases for empathy. *Neuroscientist, 17* (1), 18–24.

Sherman, G. D., Lerner, J. S., Renshon, J., Ma-Kellams, C., & Joel, S. (2015). Perceiving others' feelings: The importance of personality and social structure. *Social Psychological and Personality Science, 6* (5), 559–569.

Siegel, D. J. (2010). *Mindsight: The new science of personal transformation*. New York: Random House.

Silani, G., Lamm, C., Ruff, C. C., & Singer, T. (2013). Right supramarginal gyrus is crucial to overcome emotional egocentricity bias in social judgments. *Journal of Neuroscience, 33* (39), 15466–15476.

Silvers, J. A., Buhle, J. T., & Ochsner, K. N. (2014). The neuroscience of emotion regulation: Basic mechanisms and their role in development, aging, and psychopathology. In K. N. Ochsner & S. M. Kosslyn (Eds.), *The Oxford handbook of cognitive neuroscience*, Vol. 2: *The cutting edges*, 52–78. New York: Oxford University Press.

Singer, T. (2007). The neuronal basis of empathy and fairness. In G. Bock & J. Goode (Eds.), *Empathy and fairness*, 20–30. Hoboken, N.J.: John Wiley & Sons.

Singer, T., & Decety, J. (2011). Social neuroscience of empathy. In J. Decety & J. T. Cacioppo (Eds.), *The Oxford handbook of social neuroscience*, 551–564. New York: Oxford University Press.

Singer, T., & Klimekci, O. M. (2014). Empathy and compassion. *Current Biology*, *24* (18), R875–R878.

Singer, T., & Lamm, C. (2009). The social neuroscience of empathy. In M. Miller and A. Kingstone (Eds.), *The year in cognitive neuroscience: 2009 annals of the New York Academy of Science*, 81–96. Boston, Mass.: Blackwell.

Singer, T., Seymour, B., O'Doherty, J., Stephan, K. E., Dolan, R. J., & Frith, C. D. (2006). Empathic neural responses are modulated by the perceived fairness of others. *Nature*, *439*, 466–469.

Snowdon, C. T., & Cronin, K. A. (2009). Comparative cognition and neuroscience. In G. G. Berntson & J. T. Cacioppo (Eds.), *Handbook of neuroscience for the behavioral sciences*, 1:32–55. Hoboken, N.J.: John Wiley & Sons.

Society for Neuroscience. (2012). *BrainFacts: A primer on the brain and nervous system*. Washington, D.C.: Author.

Spreng, R. N., McKinnon, M. C., Mar, R. A., & Levine, B. (2009). The Toronto empathy questionnaire: Scale development and initial validation of a factor-analytic solution to multiple empathy measures. *Journal of Personality Assessment*, *91* (1), 62–71.

Staub, E. (2015). The roots of healing, heroic rescue and resistance to and the prevention of mass violence: Active bystandership in extreme times and in building peaceful societies. In D. A. Schroeder & W. G. Graziano (Eds.), *The Oxford handbook of prosocial behavior*, 693–717. New York: Oxford University Press.

Stone, B. L. (2008). The evolution of culture and sociology. *American Sociologist*, *39* (1), 68–85.

Stürmer, S., & Snyder, M. (2010). Helping "us" versus "them": Toward a group-level of helping and altruism within and across group boundaries. In S. Stürmer & M. Snyder (Eds.), *The psychology of prosocial behavior*, 33–58. West Sussex, U.K.: Wiley-Blackwell.

Swanson, L. W. (2012). *Brain architecture: Understanding the basic plan*, 2nd ed. New York: Oxford University Press.

Szalavitz, M., & Perry, B. D. (2010). *Born for love: Why empathy is essential—and endangered.* New York: Harper Collins.

Taylor, S. E. (2002). *The tending instinct: How nurturing is essential to who we are and how we live.* New York: Holt.

——. (2006). Tend and befriend: Biobehavioral bases of affiliation under stress. *Current Directions in Psychological Science, 15* (6), 273–277.

——. (2010). Mechanisms linking early life stress to adult health outcomes. *Proceedings of the National Academy of Science, 107* (19), 8507–8512.

Taylor, S. E., & Master, S. L. (2010). Social responses to stress: The tend-and-befriend model. In R. J. Contrada & A. Baum, (Eds.), *The handbook of stress science: Biology, psychology, and health,* 101–109. New York: Springer.

Teding van Berkhout, E., & Malouff, J. M. (2016). The efficacy of empathy training: A meta-analysis of randomized controlled trials. *Journal of Counseling Psychology, 63* (1), 32–41.

Tichener, E. (1909). *Elementary psychology of the thought processes.* New York: Macmillan.

Todd, A. R., Bodenhausen, G. V., Richeson, J. A., & Galinsky, A. D. (2011). Perspective taking combats automatic expressions of racial bias. *Journal of Personality and Social Psychology, 100* (6), 1027–1042.

Todd, R. M., & Anderson, A. K. (2014). Salience, state, and expression: The influence of specific aspects of emotion on attention and perception. In K. N. Ochsner & S. M. Kosslyn (Eds.), *The Oxford handbook of cognitive neuroscience,* Vol. 2: *The cutting edges,* 11–31. New York: Oxford University Press.

Tomova, L., von Dawans, B., Heinrichs, M., Silani, G., & Lamm, C. (2014). Is stress affecting our ability to tune into others? Evidence for gender differences in the effects of stress on self-other distinction. *Psychoneuroendocrinology, 43,* 95–104.

Tousignant, B., Eugène, F., & Jackson, P. L. (2016). A developmental perspective on the neural bases of human empathy. *Infant Behavior and Development,* in press.

Trout, J. D. (2009). *Why empathy matters: The science and psychology of better judgment.* New York: Penguin.

Turiel, E. (2015). Morality and prosocial judgments and behavior. In D. A. Schroeder & W. G. Graziano (Eds.), *The Oxford handbook of prosocial behavior,* 137–152. New York: Oxford University Press.

Turner, R. N., & Crisp, R. J. (2010). Imagining intergroup contact reduces implicit prejudice. *British Journal of Social Psychology, 49,* 129–142.

Uzefovsky, F., Shaleve, I., Israel, S., Edelman, S., Raz, Y., Mankuta, D., Knafo-Noam, A., & Ebstein, R. P. (2015). Oxytocin receptor and vasopressin receptor 1a genes are respectively associated with emotional and cognitive empathy. *Hormones and Behavior, 67,* 60–65.

van Baaren, R. B., Holland, R. W., Kawakami, K., & van Knippenberg, A. (2004). Mimicry and prosocial behavior. *Psychological Science, 15* (1), 71–74.

van Baaren, R., Janssen, L., Chartrand, T. L., & Dijksterhuis, A. (2009). Where is the love? The social aspects of mimicry. *Philosophical Transactions of the Royal Society Biological Sciences, 364,* 2381–2389.

Van Bavel, J. J., & Cunningham, W. A. (2009). Self-categorization with a novel mixed-race group moderates automatic social and racial biases. *Personality and Social Psychology Bulletin, 35* (3), 321–335.

Van Kleef, G. A., Oveis, C., Homan, A. C., van der Löwe, I., & Keltner, D. (2015). Power gets you high: The powerful are more inspired by themselves than by others. *Social Psychological and Personality Science, 6* (4), 472–480.

Vermunt, J. K. (2010). Latent class modeling with covariates: Two improved three-step approaches. *Political Analysis, 18* (4), 450–469.

Vezzali, L., Capozza, D., Stathi, S., & Giovannini, D. (2012). Increasing outgroup trust, reducing infrahumanization, and enhancing future contact intentions via imagined intergroup contact. *Journal of Experimental Social Psychology, 48,* 437–440.

Wagaman, M. A. (2011). Social empathy as a framework for adolescent empowerment. *Journal of Social Service Research, 37,* 278–293.

Waley, A. (Ed.) (1989). *The Analects of Confucius.* New York: Vintage Books.

Walter, H. (2012). Social cognitive neuroscience of empathy: Concepts, circuits, and genes. *Emotion Review, 4* (1), 9–17.

Warneken, F., & Tomasello, M. (2015). The development and evolutionary origins of human helping and sharing. In D. A. Schroeder & W. G. Graziano (Eds.), *The Oxford handbook of prosocial behavior,* 100–113. New York: Oxford University Press.

Watson, J. C. (2002). Re-visioning empathy. In D. J. Cain (Ed.), *Humanistic psychotherapies: Handbook of research and practice,* 445–471. Washington, D.C.: American Psychological Association.

Watson, J. C., & Greenberg, L. S. (2011). Empathic resonance: A neuroscience perspective. In J. Decety & W. Ickes (Eds.), *The social neuroscience of empathy,* 125–137. Cambridge, Mass.: MIT Press.

Winkielman, P., Berridge, K., & Sher, S. (2011). Emotion, consciousness, and social behavior. In J. Decety & J. T. Cacioppo (Eds.), *The Oxford handbook of social neuroscience*, 195–211. New York: Oxford University Press.

Wispé, L. (1978). Toward an integration. In L. Wispé (Ed.), *Altruisim, sympathy, and helping: Psychological and sociological principles*, 303–328. New York: Academic Press.

——. (1986). History of the concept of empathy. In N. Eisenberg & J. Strayer (Eds.), *Empathy and its development*, 17–37. Cambridge, U.K.: Cambridge University Press.

Wolf, O. T., Schulte, J. M., Drimalla, H., Hamacher-Dang, T. C., Knoch, D., & Dziobek, I. (2015). Enhanced emotional empathy after psychosocial stress in young healthy men. *Stress, 18* (6), 631–637.

Xu, X., Zuo, X., Wang, X., & Han, S. (2009). Do you feel my pain? Racial group membership modulates empathic neural responses. *Journal of Neuroscience, 29* (26), 8525–8529.

Yang, S. G., & Hugenberg, K. (2010). Mere social categorization modulates identification of facial expressions of emotion. *Journal of Personality and Social Psychology, 99*, 964–977.

Yao, S., Becker, B., Geng, Y., Zhao, Z., Xu, X., Zhao, W., Ren, P., & Kendrick, K. M. (2016). Voluntary control of anterior insula and its functional connections is feedback-independent and increases pain empathy. *NeuroImage, 130*, 230–240.

Young, L., & Waytz, A. (2013). Mind attribution is for morality. In S. Baron-Cohen, H. Tager-Flusberg, & M. V. Lombardo (Eds.), *Understanding other minds*, 93–103. New York: Oxford University Press.

Young, S.G. & Hugenberg, K. (2010). Mere socialization categorization modulates identification of facial expressions of emotion. *Journal of Personality and Social Psychology, 99* (6), 964–977.

Zahavi, D. (2012). Basic empathy and complex empathy. *Emotion Review*, (1), 81–82.

Zaki, J., & Ochsner, K. (2012). The neuroscience of empathy: Progress, pitfalls, and promise. *Nature Neuroscience, 15* (5), 675–680.

——. (2013). Neural sources of empathy: An evolving story. In S. Baron-Cohen, H. Tager-Flusberg, & M. V. Lombardo (Eds.), *Understanding other minds: Perspectives from developmental social neuroscience*, 214–232. New York: Oxford University Press.

Zhou, Q., Eisenberg, N., Losoy, S. H., Fabes, R. A., Reiser, M., Guthrie, I. K., Murphy, B. C., Cumberland, A. J. & Shepard, S. A. (2002). The relations of parental warmth and positive expressiveness to children's empathy-related responding and social functioning: A longitudinal study. *Child Development*, *73* (3), 893–915.

CPSIA information can be obtained
at www.ICGtesting.com
Printed in the USA
JSHW011609240720
6888JS00001B/59